Everyday Nervous System Regulation

Everyday **Nervous System Regulation**

Simple Exercises to Reset & Recenter

Melissa Romano, LGSW

ZEITGEIST • NEW YORK

For anyone who's ever wondered, *What's wrong with me, why am I like this, and how do I make it stop?!* And for my son, whose existence rewires my nervous system daily.

Zeitgeist™
An imprint and division of Penguin Random House LLC
1745 Broadway, New York, NY 10019
zeitgeistpublishing.com
penguinrandomhouse.com

ISBN: 9798217331130
Ebook ISBN: 9798217330836

Printed in the United States of America
1st Printing

Illustrations by Kate Francis
Book design by Katy Brown
Author photograph © by Donnie Shilling
Edited by Erin Nelson

The authorized representative in the EU for product safety and compliance is Penguin Random House Ireland, Morrison Chambers, 32 Nassau Street, Dublin D02 YH68, Ireland. https://eu-contact.penguin.ie

Safety Disclaimer

A quick note before we dive in: This book is meant to be educational and supportive, not a replacement for medical or mental-health care. If you're dealing with ongoing pain, dizziness, trouble breathing, or emotional overwhelm that feels unmanageable, please reach out to a qualified professional. When trying practices that involve temperature changes, breath work, or movement, trust your body and adjust as needed. You know yourself best.

If you're pregnant (especially past 20 weeks), or have back or spinal concerns, use caution with exercises that involve lying flat on your back and consult your healthcare provider as needed.

Attribution and Respect

Many of these practices draw from wisdom traditions and lineages from around the world. I'm a white woman sharing knowledge that comes from many different cultures and communities, and I want to be honest about that. I can't capture the full depth and richness of these traditions here, and I'm definitely not claiming to be an expert in them. When I know where something comes from, I'll tell you, but regardless of what I know or don't know about their origins, I share all these practices with deep respect and gratitude for the teachers and communities who have kept this wisdom alive.

Contents

PART III: PRACTICE PLANS AND PERSONALIZATION

Introduction

If you've picked up this book, great news: We're officially in this together. Maybe your brain feels like it's running a marathon while everyone else is taking a leisurely stroll. Maybe sleep feels like negotiating with a toddler who doesn't want to go to bed. Maybe your stomach has its own opinions about everything, or your energy swings from 0 to 100 with no in-between, or your body has learned to brace for impact even when you're just standing in line at the grocery store. Or maybe you're simply curious: Is there actually a way to feel better from the inside out?

There is. Here's the thing about regulation: It's not about being calm all the time or having your life perfectly together. It's about staying connected to yourself, others, and the present moment, even when life gets messy. Your nervous system touches everything: digestion, immunity, energy, focus, mood, sleep, relationships, creativity, and so on. When your stress response gets stuck in the "on" position, the world starts to feel smaller and scarier. When your nervous system can shift and adapt, possibilities open up.

You don't need anything to be "wrong" with you to benefit from what's ahead. Nothing about you needs fixing. Most of the time, we're struggling because our nervous system is working too hard, not because it's broken. We're not chasing some zen-like state of perpetual calm here. We're learning to work with what we've got, listen to our body's signals, and remember that we have choices in how we respond to life.

I came to this work the hard way (my favorite way to learn), through my own nervous system adventures, years of professional training, and supporting countless clients who felt "too much," "not enough," or just plain exhausted from trying to think their way out of what's rooted in the body. My background in social work and nervous system work meets you here, in plain language that applies to your everyday life.

Every exercise in this book works with pathways you already have: breath, movement, sound, touch, rhythm, relationship, and nature. You came equipped with factory settings. Relief can happen quickly; recovery is the longer game, built from gentle repetition that helps your system remember what safety feels like.

You're not behind. You're not broken. You're here, and that's exactly where you need to be.

What You'll Find in This Book

This book is organized into three parts:

Part I: Foundations. We'll explore how your nervous system works and why it matters, without drowning you in science jargon. You'll understand just enough to stop blaming yourself and start working with your body instead of against it.

Part II: Everyday Exercises. You'll find an emergency toolkit with 10 quick resets for when you need help but don't know where to start, followed by 90 simple, research-backed practices organized by how you're feeling right now: frozen, anxious, angry, off, needing sleep, or craving connection. Each practice follows the same friendly template, and at least 10 percent use nature as your co-regulation partner.

Part III: Practice Plans and Personalization. This includes a seven-day reset plan, a 30-day resilience builder, and step-by-step guidance to create your own approach that fits your actual life—your schedule, constraints, and what feels sustainable.

How to Use This Book

Flip to what you need right now or read straight through. There's no wrong way to use this book. Your nervous system is unique, which means there's no single "right" way to regulate. You can browse by how you're feeling, open to a random page, or work chapter by chapter. If you're not sure where to start, try the Emergency Toolkit in chapter 3, 10 quick practices that work across all nervous system states.

If you like structure, part III offers two ready-made options: a seven-day reset that builds relief into your morning, midday, and evening, and a 30-day resilience builder for longer-term change. From there, chapter 12 helps you create a plan that fits into your life.

Track what helps and what doesn't. See what surprises you. Make exercises shorter or longer. Combine practices you love. Skip what doesn't feel quite right. Rigidity is the opposite of regulation.

Most importantly, be gentle with yourself. Even 30 seconds counts. Small, repeated signals create bigger shifts over time. If you miss a day or a week, you haven't failed—you're human. Pick up where you left off.

You already have wisdom. Let's help you access it.

What This Book Is (and Isn't)

WHAT IT IS

- **Accessible.** You do not need special equipment, workout clothes, or meditation cushions. These practices meet you wherever you are—at your desk, in your car, on a walk, or even in your bed.
- **Trauma informed.** The exercises honor your body's protective responses rather than treating them as problems to eliminate. You are invited to notice, adjust, and choose what works for you. There is no "should" or requirement to push past what's safe.
- **Whole-person focused.** Your mind, body, and spirit are all considered here. I apply tools that use evidence-based approaches and traditions from around the world, while respectfully acknowledging their origins.
- **A meaningful place to begin.** This isn't about willpower or becoming perfectly calm. It's a practical companion for both relief (right now) and recovery (over time).

WHAT IT ISN'T

- **A diagnosis or a cure-all.** These practices don't replace medical or mental-health care. If you're dealing with ongoing pain, medical concerns, or significant emotional stress, please work with qualified professionals.
- **A call for perfect routines or gold stars.** Your nervous system learns through gentle, repeated experiences of safety, not through self-judgment or pressure.
- **A one-size-fits-all.** You're invited to adapt, skip, and remix everything. The right practice is whatever your body can say yes to today.

PART I
Foundations

This part introduces the landscape of your nervous system and what happens when it's pushed outside its comfort zone. You'll learn how your body protects you, why dysregulation happens, and what it means to regulate. These chapters aren't science lessons to memorize; they're guides to help you understand what's happening inside and begin your own practice with compassion.

CHAPTER 1

Understanding Your Nervous System

Your phone buzzes with an unknown number or a name that activates you, or worse, your doorbell unexpectedly rings. In milliseconds, your heart rate shifts, your breathing changes, and your attention . . . well, are you even in charge anymore?! You haven't consciously decided to feel alert or worried; your nervous system has already assessed the situation and responded. This automatic process, happening beneath your awareness thousands of times daily, determines whether you feel safe enough to connect, create, and engage, or whether you need to protect, withdraw, or prepare for action.

This isn't about managing anxiety or achieving calm. It's about understanding that your nervous system operates through states of connection and disconnection, constantly scanning for safety and threat. When it detects safety, through predictable routines, trusted relationships, or internal coherence, it maintains regulation that supports social engagement. When it perceives danger, it disconnects you from overwhelming stimuli through mobilization or shutdown. These responses aren't personal failings; they're biological imperatives shaped by evolution and experience.

The practical question isn't how to eliminate nervous system responses but how to work with them intelligently.

A Closer Look at the Stress Cycle

Your body's stress response is one of nature's most sophisticated survival mechanisms. When you encounter a threat—whether it's a speeding car or a heated argument—your nervous system immediately mobilizes energy to help you respond. Your heart pumps faster, muscles engage, and stress hormones course through your system. This isn't a malfunction or weakness; it's your body demonstrating remarkable intelligence, preparing you to meet whatever challenge lies ahead.

Under ideal conditions, this activation naturally transitions into completion and recovery. Once you've navigated the situation, your body discharges the mobilized energy—through movement, vocalization, shaking, or even a good cry—and gradually returns to baseline. Think of how animals in the wild shake after escaping a predator, then calmly return to grazing. This complete cycle allows your system to process the experience and reset.

Modern life, however, often interrupts this natural completion. We face chronic stressors without clear resolution, suppress our responses to maintain social appropriateness, or carry unresolved experiences that keep our system on high alert. When stress energy can't complete its cycle, we become dysregulated.

Dysregulation isn't a diagnosis; it's a state that looks different for everyone. You might feel anxious and restless, or heavy and disconnected. You might swing from feeling everything intensely to feeling nothing at all. These responses aren't signs of failure; they're evidence your nervous system is working hard to protect you.

SIGNS OF DYSREGULATION

While not an exhaustive list, signs of dysregulation may include:

Physical: Racing heart, shallow breathing, muscle tension, digestive issues, fatigue, restlessness, feeling "wired but tired"

Emotional: Feeling overwhelmed or numb, mood swings, increased irritability, difficulty accessing joy or excitement

Mental: Racing thoughts, difficulty concentrating, brain fog, rumination, catastrophic thinking

Behavioral: Sleep disruption, changes in appetite, social withdrawal, increased conflict, difficulty making decisions, procrastination or hyperproductivity

Relational: Feeling disconnected from others, difficulty trusting, increased reactivity in relationships, feeling like you're "too much" or "not enough"

WHAT'S HAPPENING IN THE BODY

Every thought, emotion, and stress response begins with a conversation between your central nervous system and your autonomic nervous system. The central nervous system is made up of your brain and spinal cord. It processes information, interprets what's happening around you, makes decisions, forms thoughts and emotions, and sends instructions to the rest of your body. If your nervous system was an organization, the central nervous system would be the headquarters.

The autonomic nervous system, then, is your body's behind-the-scenes manager that takes care of everything you don't have to think about—your heartbeat, breathing, digestion, and countless other processes that keep you functioning. It's always on, always working, and constantly adjusting based on what's happening around you and inside you. If the central nervous system interprets your experience, the autonomic nervous system carries out the response.

Within the autonomic nervous system, there are two main branches. Simply put, the sympathetic nervous system mobilizes you and the parasympathetic nervous system restores you. For decades, we've talked about stress in terms of fight or flight, as if your nervous system had an on-off switch. But polyvagal theory reveals something that more closely aligns with our lived experiences: The autonomic nervous system operates more like a highway with three lanes, each with its own purpose and intelligence.

When you feel safe and connected, you're cruising in your **safe-and-social lane** (your ventral vagal system—one pathway of the parasympathetic branch). This is where you feel grounded, playful, and genuinely present with others. You can think clearly, laugh easily, and handle life's curveballs without getting completely derailed. Being in this lane doesn't mean you feel only pleasant emotions. You can experience sadness, disappointment, or frustration while still feeling connected to yourself and others. The difference is that these emotions move through you rather than overwhelming or shutting you down.

As social mammals, we've evolved with a remarkable capacity for co-regulation, which means our nervous systems naturally influence and sync with one another. Co-regulation is one of the beautiful options we've evolved to have for finding safety and connection. Sometimes, though, our nervous system develops protective responses like codependency, where we lose ourselves trying to manage someone else's emotions or need them to be okay for us to be okay.

When your system detects threat or stress, it merges into the **fight-or-flight lane** (sympathetic). Here you feel anxious, angry, urgent, or activated. Your body is mobilizing energy to meet whatever challenge lies ahead. This isn't pathology; it's intelligent preparation.

If the threat feels too overwhelming or inescapable, your system can shift into the **freeze-or-shutdown lane** (dorsal vagal—the other pathway within the parasympathetic branch). This is where you might feel shutdown, spacey, hopeless, or numb. Your body essentially hits the brakes to conserve energy and protect you from further overwhelm.

A quick note on polyvagal theory. If you've heard that it has been "debunked," here's what's actually going on: Scientists are debating the precise mechanics of *how* the vagus nerve works, not its existence or importance. But no one is disputing that our bodies experience fight, flight, freeze, and shutdown responses.

Think of it this way: science is the map, your body is the territory. And maps are never as detailed as the actual terrain. No single theory can capture every mechanism in your body but polyvagal theory gives us the language for how we understand trauma and the body. The current debate doesn't undo that. If anything, it just proves what we already know: our bodies are more complex than any framework can fully explain.

Another crucial point to understand: Moving from collapse back to safety means passing through activation because the two branches of your autonomic nervous system—sympathetic and parasympathetic—are always in communication with each other. The sympathetic branch mobilizes you (fight or flight), while the parasympathetic branch has two pathways—one that helps you rest and connect (ventral vagal) and one that shuts you down when overwhelmed (dorsal vagal). This explains why you might sit down to meditate when you're feeling shutdown and want to crawl out of your skin within minutes. You're not broken—you're moving from dorsal shutdown through sympathetic activation on your way back to ventral connection, and that often involves a temporary period of feeling agitated or restless. This isn't a step backward; it's your system's natural path to recovery.

Remember, your nervous system doesn't differentiate between a charging bear and a harsh email from your boss. It responds to patterns and predictions based on your past experiences, often reacting before you're consciously aware that anything has shifted.

This isn't something you can simply think your way out of or control through willpower. Your nervous system is doing precisely what it was designed to do: keep you alive and help you navigate the world as safely as possible. It does this even if what it perceives as safe, simply because it's familiar, is now keeping you stuck.

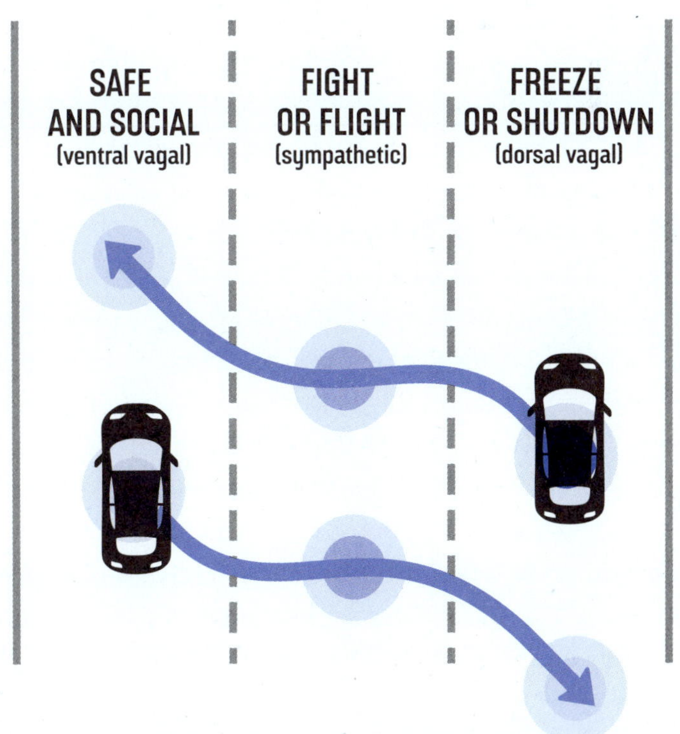

OTHER SURVIVAL RESPONSES

Beyond fight, flight, and freeze, humans adapt in other ways:

- **Fawn/appease:** pleasing others to avoid conflict
- **Submit:** complying or collapsing autonomy under pressure
- **Tend and befriend:** seeking connection or nurturing in order to survive stress
- **Attach/cry for help:** reaching out in desperation, clinging, or protesting

Each is a form of self-protection. Regulation doesn't mean erasing them. It means reclaiming choice, including the choice to set boundaries, ask for help, or rest.

WHAT IS THE VAGUS NERVE?

The vagus nerve is your body's information superhighway, the longest cranial nerve that wanders (that's what "vagus" means) from your brainstem through your torso, connecting with all your major organs along the way. If your nervous system organization had a gossip, this would be it.

Here's what makes it fascinating: About 80 percent of the vagus nerve's fibers are sensory afferent, meaning they're constantly sending updates to your brain about what's happening in your body, rather than waiting for instructions from above. Your vagus nerve is basically that friend who keeps you in the loop about everything: your heart rate, breathing, digestion, inflammation levels, and all those subtle internal sensations that help you know when you're hungry, tired, or need to use the bathroom. This internal awareness is called interoception, and it's how your brain stays informed about your body's needs and state.

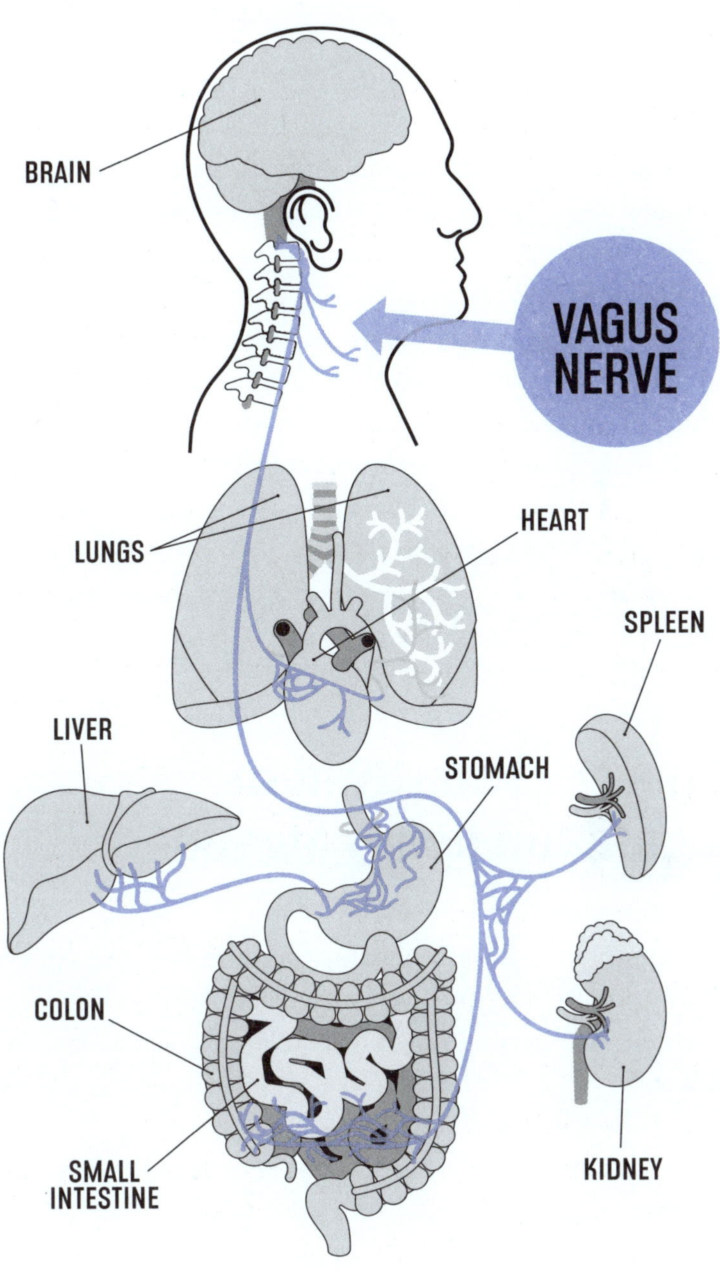
BRAIN
VAGUS NERVE
LUNGS
HEART
SPLEEN
LIVER
STOMACH
COLON
SMALL INTESTINE
KIDNEY

This nerve plays a starring role in both your autonomic nervous system and immune function. When your vagus nerve is well toned, meaning it's strong, responsive, and flexible, it helps keep inflammation in check, facilitates ease of digestion, and allows your nervous system to transition smoothly between activation and rest. Think of vagal toning like gentle exercise for your nervous system.

In the short term, activating your vagus nerve is like hitting a reset button that helps you feel more grounded and responsive in the moment. Long term, it builds your resilience and ability to both handle and bounce back from stress. Because this communication flows primarily from body to brain, you can't just think your way into better vagal tone; your body needs to lead the conversation. The exercises in this book are designed to help you have exactly that kind of dialogue.

What Nervous System Regulation Really Means

Here's the truth—regulated means connected, not calm. Nervous system regulation is about staying connected to yourself, others, and the present moment, even when life gets messy.

When your nervous system is regulated, you can feel angry without losing yourself in rage, sad without disappearing into despair, or excited without spinning into anxiety. You remain connected to your body's signals, your emotions, and your ability to think clearly and make choices. You can feel the full range of human experiences while maintaining your sense of self and your capacity for connecting with others.

Physically, this shows up as your body being able to respond to what's *actually* happening rather than what it thinks *might* happen. Your heart might race during a job interview, then settle afterward. Your breathing might quicken when you're excited, then slow when you're relaxed. Your body moves with life instead of staying stuck in one gear.

From the inside out, regulation feels like having options and staying present with whatever arises. Instead of automatically reacting from old patterns, you can pause, feel what's happening, and choose how to respond. Some days you'll feel more sensitive or reactive than others, and that's completely natural. Our nervous systems are designed to shift and adapt throughout the day. The goal is to stay connected through these natural fluctuations and find your way back to safety and presence when you're ready.

WHY REGULATION MATTERS

Understanding what regulation feels like from the inside is just the beginning. Regulation is the secret sauce for optimal digestion, sleep, and immune function. Who knew that feeling safe could be such good medicine?

But here's where it gets interesting. Regulation affects your ability to be creative, take risks, and be authentic in relationships. When you're connected to yourself, you can actually listen to your partner without planning your defense strategy. You can express your needs without a 20-minute disclaimer about how you're not being demanding.

Regulation also unlocks your capacity for joy and wonder. When your nervous system feels safe, you can notice the way the light hits the window, actually taste your coffee instead of just drinking it, or feel your shoulders drop without reminding yourself to breathe.

Learning your own regulation patterns is like rewriting your story. When you understand how your nervous system works, you can finally stop fighting against your own biology and start working with it instead.

RELIEF AND RECOVERY

This story you're rewriting unfolds in two important ways: relief and recovery. Relief is the immediate reset you feel when you try one of the exercises in this book. It's that exhale after a long day, the moment your shoulders drop, or when your racing thoughts finally slow down. Relief happens in real time and reminds your body that safety is possible right now.

Recovery is the deeper work of building resilience and strengthening your vagus nerve over time. It's what happens when you practice these exercises consistently, allowing your body to gradually exit chronic states of hypervigilance—that low-grade alarm system that's been running in the background for years. Recovery contributes to long-term, systemic healing as your nervous system remembers what regulation feels like and gets better at finding its way back there.

You may have learned at some point that your body stores trauma. Well, your body stores relief and recovery too, creating new neural pathways that become more consistent and easier to access over time. Every moment of relief you experience teaches your nervous system something valuable about safety and connection.

The exercises in this book are designed to give you both. Some will offer immediate relief when you're spinning out or shutting down. Others will slowly but surely strengthen your overall capacity for regulation. You don't have to choose between feeling better right now and healing for the long haul; your nervous system is smart enough to do both.

CHAPTER 2

Getting Started with Everyday Practice

Now that you have a broader view of how your nervous system works, let's talk about how to put this knowledge to use in your daily life. This chapter is your gentle guide to building a personal regulation practice that fits your real life, not some idealized version of it.

You won't find rigid schedules or complicated protocols here. Instead, you'll discover the power of "a little bit and often"—tiny moments of regulation sprinkled throughout your day rather than carving out perfect 30-minute blocks. Think: washing your hands mindfully, taking three conscious breaths before a meeting, or doing a quick body scan while your coffee brews.

If consistency isn't a strong neural pathway for you yet, give yourself permission to be inconsistent to start. Your nervous system learns through repetition, but it also learns through kindness. Building trust with your body matters more than checking boxes on a routine. Some days you'll remember these practices; other days you won't. Both are part of learning to work with your unique rhythm.

An Exercise in Reflection

Here's the thing about nervous system regulation: It requires reflection, and reflection is harder than it sounds. When was the last time you paused to ask yourself, "What am I feeling right now? What does my body need?" If you're drawing a blank, welcome to the club. Learning to check in with yourself (identifying sensations, emotions, needs, and reactions) is a critical part of any healing journey. It's also a muscle that gets stronger with practice, in small moments, over time.

This is where the structure of this book becomes your friend. Try flipping to the tools that match your current state. Angry? Overwhelmed? Disconnected? Whatever you're experiencing, there's a chapter for that. This simple act of connecting what you feel to what might help develops that reflection muscle we're talking about. And here's the relief: There is no wrong tool or wrong answer. Your body knows what it needs, even when your mind feels confused.

If you're having trouble identifying what you need, that's completely normal, especially when you've been running on empty for a while. Your internal signals might feel scrambled or muted right now. The exercises in this book will still reset your body-mind-spirit connection even when you can't name what's happening. When in doubt, start with the Emergency Toolkit in chapter 3. These tools work across all nervous system states and can help you find your way back to yourself.

LET IT BE MESSY!

As you're building that reflection muscle, let it be messy. Nervous system regulation isn't always about focusing or calming down. Sometimes the kindest thing you can do is not meditate when you're anxious or not go for a run when you're frozen.

Your nervous system has its own logic, and part of that "little bit and often" approach is learning to tune in to what it actually needs rather than what you think it should need. When you're anxious, your system often craves downshifting tools that help you ground, soothe, and discharge all that buzzy energy. When you're shutdown, you might need gentle upshifting practices that stimulate and reconnect without overwhelming you. When you're angry, safe expression becomes key—channeling and releasing rather than stuffing it down.

IDENTIFYING PATTERNS

As you experiment with these practices, become a gentle detective of your own experience:

- **Before:** What do you feel right now? Buzzy? Heavy? Scattered? Angry?
- **After:** What shifted? Did your shoulders drop? Did your breathing slow? Do you feel more like yourself?
- **Track:** Which exercises work best for different moods or times of day?

This creates a feedback loop that helps you learn what works for your unique nervous system. Approach this investigation with curiosity, not judgment. Some days a practice might feel amazing; other days it might do nothing. Both responses give you valuable information for building your personalized toolkit.

The exercises in this book are organized around these different states because your body already knows what it needs. These practices just help you listen and tune in more clearly. You're not trying to override your nervous system or force yourself into someone else's idea of wellness. You're learning to work with your own rhythm, even when that rhythm feels chaotic or unpredictable.

So here it is, your permission slip: Be messy, be inconsistent, trust your instincts, and let your nervous system guide you toward what feels good.

Regulation Is Rhythmic

Your nervous system is basically obsessed with rhythm. Your heartbeat, your breathing, the way you naturally rock when you're upset or sway when you're content—none of this is coincidental. Rhythm feels safe to your body because it's predictable, and predictability tells your nervous system that all is well.

This shows up everywhere around you too. The sun rises and sets, seasons change, waves crash in patterns, and even your morning coffee routine has a rhythm to it. When life feels chaotic, these predictable patterns become little anchors of safety.

The exercises in this book tap into the rhythms of your body and the natural world. Some involve tapping, humming, or gentle swaying. Others use the steady in and out of your breath or simple repetitive movements. There's nothing fancy or mystical—well, nothing fancier or more mystical than you already are—just working with the patterns your nervous system already loves and using them to help you feel more like yourself again.

FINDING YOUR OWN REGULATION RHYTHMS

Rhythm does not equal routine. Here's the thing: You don't need a routine, but it helps. Before you panic about adding one more item to your already packed schedule, let me be clear. This isn't about creating rigid structure or perfect consistency. Your nervous system does not like the whole "here's a list of 25 things I will start or stop doing by a certain date" approach at all. It finds that overwhelming, and frankly, it will rebel like a teenager who's been told to clean their room, do their homework, and be home by 10 p.m. all in the same breath.

Instead, this is about noticing the natural rhythms you already have and gently inviting some nervous system support into those moments. These existing pockets of time are perfect for tiny regulation practices. The secret is anchoring small practices to things you already do—for example: "I will do three shoulder rolls before I brush my teeth," "I will hum in the car on the way to work," or "I will take two conscious breaths before I check my phone." Think micro-routines.

Remember, these rhythms will change with the seasons, literally and figuratively. Your routine with a newborn looks very different from your routine with a 10-year-old. Your winter practices might feel completely different from your summer ones. The goal is to slip these practices into the flow of your day rather than forcing your day to accommodate them. Like brushing your teeth or driving a car, these practices become more natural the more you do them, adapting and evolving as your life does.

SUPPORTING YOUR RHYTHMS, IN PRACTICE

Now that you're thinking about rhythms instead of rigid routines, here are some ways to support yourself as you begin experimenting with nervous system regulation:

A little and often. Remember that "little bit and often" approach we talked about? It applies here too. Even 30 seconds of these exercises can start rewiring how your system responds to stress. Your nervous system learns through safety, not force, so gentleness becomes part of the healing itself. Think of it like coaxing a nervous cat out from under the bed rather than trying to drag it out.

Repetition over intensity. Your nervous system craves repetition, not intensity. Doing something imperfectly three times a week beats doing it perfectly once and then burning out. Your brain builds new pathways through practice, not perfection.

Find what feels good. Not what looks good on social media or what worked for your best friend or what some wellness guru says you should do. Maybe meditation makes you want to crawl out of your skin, but humming in the shower feels like magic. Maybe yoga feels too slow, but two minutes of kitchen dancing resets your entire day. Trust your body's feedback over anyone else's recommendations.

Create a sensory anchor. Set up a small space or portable kit with things that help you feel regulated. This could be a cozy corner with a soft blanket and your favorite candle, or a little collection of items that ground you. I keep a specific crystal and a little bag with my favorite scents at home, plus a palo santo roller in my purse and a photo of my son in my wallet for when I'm out and about.

Your sensory anchor doesn't need to make sense to anyone else. Maybe yours is a playlist that instantly calms you, a piece of fabric from an old T-shirt, or the smell of a particular hand lotion. Some people need visual anchors like fairy lights or a view out the window. Others crave textures like worry stones or fidget toys. The goal is having reliable sensory experiences that signal safety to your nervous system, whether you're at home or stuck in a waiting room. Trust what works for you, even if it seems random. Your body knows what it needs.

WHAT TO DO WHEN YOU MISS A DAY (OR WEEKS)

Let's address the elephant in the room: You're going to forget about these practices sometimes. Maybe for a day, maybe for three weeks, maybe until you find this book again under a pile of laundry. Or you'll just knowingly be like "Nope, not today." This is not a character flaw or a sign that nervous system regulation doesn't work for you. It's just being human.

Consistency has its benefits; it helps build those neural pathways we talked about. But spontaneity has value too. Sometimes your body needs a break from structure, or life gets messy and these practices fall off your radar entirely. Both consistency and spontaneity serve your nervous system in different ways.

Here's what you need to know: There's no such thing as falling behind. You can't undo the relief and repair you've already experienced. When you're ready to return to these practices, your body will remember. It's like riding a bike. The muscle memory is still there, even if it feels a little wobbly at first.

You can always pick up exactly where you left off. No need to start over, no need to punish yourself, no need to do extra to make up for lost time. Just open the book, try a practice that feels good, and trust that your body is happy to have you back.

The Exercises, Explained

Before you dive into part II, let's talk about how these exercises are set up so you know what to expect. Every practice in this book follows the same friendly template, which means once you get the hang of one, the rest will feel familiar.

Each exercise starts with the quick science behind why this particular practice works. It's included because your brain likes to understand what's happening in and around you.

It's followed by a **Use This When** entry. Think of this as a gentle suggestion, not a strict prescription. It's more like "Hey, this might be helpful if you're feeling this way" rather than "You must only do this exercise under these exact circumstances."

Then comes the simple steps you can follow even when your brain feels like scrambled eggs. Nothing complicated, no special equipment needed.

Finally, **Make It Yours** is where things get fun. These are ways to adapt each exercise to fit your body, your space, and your life. Maybe you need it quieter, bigger, shorter, or completely different. Your call.

The whole point is making these practices so doable that they feel second nature.

A QUICK LOOK AT THE MODALITIES AT PLAY

Each exercise is driven by one or more of the modalities below. You can think of modalities as the different languages your nervous system speaks.

- **Movement:** using your body to shift energy or activate your proprioceptive system which helps bring awareness back into your body
- **Breath:** working with breathing rhythm to signal safety or alertness
- **Sound:** humming, sighing, or vocalizing to release tension
- **Touch:** using pressure or texture to ground your nervous system
- **Ritual:** creating meaningful sequences for comfort and transition
- **Co-regulation:** connecting with others, pets, or nature
- **Sensory orientation:** using your senses to anchor in the present

Your nervous system might respond better to certain modalities depending on your current state. There's no hierarchy; they're just different tools for helping you feel more like yourself.

The Tools You Already Have

Here's something beautiful: You're not starting from scratch. You're coming to this with a fully-fledged toolkit that's been with you your whole life:

- Your breath has been regulating you since your first inhale.
- Your body has an incredible capacity for movement, stillness, and everything in between.
- You have access to an outdoor space; if there's fresh air, it counts. Even a fire escape or a cracked window will do.
- You have rhythm in your heartbeat, your walk, and even in the way you pace or rock.
- You have relationships—with people, pets, plants, or even the memory of someone who made you feel safe.

These aren't just nice-to-haves; they're the foundation of every exercise in this book. The fancy stuff is optional. The expensive equipment is unnecessary. What you need, you already carry with you.

When you're ready to move from relief to recovery—from trying these exercises occasionally to building them into your life—part III is waiting for you. Chapter 11 offers ready-made seven-day and 30-day plans you can start immediately. Chapter 12 helps you track what works and create your own personalized approach. But for now, just remember that you came equipped with factory settings. Everything you need to begin is already yours.

You Don't Have to Heal Alone

Humans are literally wired to regulate together, and that doesn't just mean with other humans. Your nervous system can co-regulate with pets while feeling the rhythm of a cat's purr, listening to the steady breathing of a sleeping dog, or even watching fish swim in a tank. You can co-regulate with nature too by sitting next to water and listening to its flow, watching birds from your window, seeing the wind move through trees, feeling the sun on your face, or spending time with plants in your home or garden.

If you have access to safe human relationships, lean into them. This might look like therapy or group work if that's available to you, friendships where you can just be, or creative communities where you feel seen. But if connection feels hard or unsafe right now, start with what's available. Maybe it's spending time with a pet, sitting outside where you can sense other living things, watching clouds drift by, tending to houseplants, or even talking to the tree outside your window. Chapter 9 focuses specifically on connection and co-regulation exercises. The truth is, you don't have to heal in complete isolation. There are living systems all around you that can help your nervous system remember what connection feels like. Start exactly where you are. And remember, I'm with you, and so is everyone else reading this book.

PART II

Everyday Exercises

Welcome to the heart of this book. These are everyday tools for relief and reconnection, organized by how you're actually feeling rather than some theoretical progression you're supposed to follow. You don't need to know the exact label for your nervous system state; just notice what's happening in your body. Feeling frozen? Flip to chapter 4. Anxious and spinning? Try chapter 7. Not sure where to start? Begin with the Emergency Toolkit in chapter 3.

You don't need to work through these chapters in order. Your nervous system doesn't move in straight lines, so neither does this part of the book. The chapters loosely follow the pathway from dysregulation to safety and connection, but you get to choose your own entry point based on what your body is telling you right now.

Pick what feels right, try what sounds doable, and trust that every small practice contributes to your system learning what regulation feels like.

CHAPTER 3

The Emergency Toolkit—10 Quick Resets

This chapter is your safety net. These are 10 simple, powerful tools that work across all nervous system states, whether you're shutdown, spinning, or somewhere in between. They're designed to be safe, accessible, and beginner-friendly—the kind of practices you can do anytime, anywhere, even when your brain feels too scattered to make decisions.

Not sure what you need? Start here. Pick one at random. Try whatever catches your eye. These exercises don't require you to know what state you're in or what's wrong. They just work. Think of this as your way in when everything else feels too complicated or overwhelming.

You can return to this chapter again and again, or use it as a launching pad to explore the more specific practices in the chapters ahead. There's no wrong way to use these tools.

Voo Sound

The low-pitched sound stimulates the vagus nerve through vocal vibration and breath control. It also brings awareness back into the body and invites gentle engagement with the environment, helping to shift from shutdown toward a more regulated state.

Use When: You need a quick reset, feel disconnected from your body, or want to gently activate your nervous system.

1. Sit comfortably with your feet on the ground.
2. Inhale gently through your nose.
3. As you exhale, make a deep *vooooooo* sound, like a cow mooing or a low foghorn, for as long as you can.
4. Feel the vibration in your chest or belly.
5. Pause, then repeat 3 to 5 times.

MAKE IT YOURS

- Try doing it lying down with a blanket over you if sitting feels too exposed.
- Combine with light rocking or swaying to add rhythmic movement.
- Experiment with the pitch; lower tones tend to create more vibration in the chest and belly.

Bilateral Lap Taps

Bilateral stimulation helps integrate the left and right hemispheres of your brain, creating a calming effect. The rhythm provides predictability and safety signals to your nervous system, while the physical touch brings you back into your body.

Use When: You need to ground quickly, want to feel more present in your body, or need a simple reset.

1. Sit comfortably with your hands resting on your thighs.
2. Begin tapping your right hand on your right thigh, then your left hand on your left thigh.
3. Continue alternating in a steady rhythm, like a slow heartbeat.
4. Let your eyes stay open or gently closed, whatever feels comfortable.
5. Keep tapping for 1 to 2 minutes, or until you notice a shift in your body.

MAKE IT YOURS

- Speed it up if you're feeling sluggish or need more activation.
- Slow it down if you're feeling anxious or overwhelmed.
- Add counting to each tap if your mind needs more focus.

Grounding Down

Pressing your feet into the ground activates proprioceptive receptors, sensory nerves that tell your brain where your body is in space, which send signals of stability and safety to your brain. This simple pressure helps orient you in space and reminds your nervous system that you're supported and grounded.

Use When: You need to ground quickly, feel disconnected from your body, or want to feel more stable.

1. Sit or stand with both feet flat on the ground.
2. Press your feet firmly into the floor, as if you're trying to make an impression.
3. Notice the sensation of the ground beneath you, the pressure in your feet.
4. Hold the press for 5 to 10 seconds, then release.
5. Repeat 3 to 5 times, noticing how your body feels more anchored with each press.

MAKE IT YOURS

- Try this barefoot, if possible, to increase sensory input.
- Combine with taking a deep breath each time you press.
- Do this standing if you need more activation or sitting if you need to be subtle.

Color Hunt

Actively searching for and naming colors pulls your attention out of your internal spiral and into the present moment, and brings your prefrontal cortex—the thinking, decision-making part of your brain—back online. Your brain can't be fully consumed by anxiety while it's engaged in a visual task, giving your nervous system a brief reset.

Use When: Your thoughts are racing, you feel overwhelmed, or you need to shift your focus outward.

1. Pause wherever you are and look around your environment.
2. Find something red. Really look at it. Notice its shade, texture, and where it sits.
3. Find something blue. Take a moment to observe it fully.
4. Find something yellow, then green, then one more color of your choice.
5. Notice how your breathing and thoughts have shifted.

MAKE IT YOURS

- Choose any five colors that feel easy to find in your space.
- Try finding five shades of the same color for a different challenge.
- Touch each colored object as you find it to add tactile grounding.

Temperature Reset

Temperature is one of the fastest ways to shift your nervous system state. Cool temperatures can help when you're feeling overheated or activated, while warmth can soothe when you're feeling tense or shutdown. The sensory input gives your brain something concrete to focus on. Use what's available: ice cubes, warm laundry, cold food, or a heated car seat. Notice which temperature your body craves in this moment.

Use When: You need an immediate shift, feel stuck in your head, or want to change your physical state quickly.

1. Find something cool (e.g., a glass of water, metal doorknob, or cold window) or warm (e.g., mug of tea, heating pad, or your own neck).
2. Place your hand on it and keep it there for at least 30 seconds.
3. Notice the temperature spreading through your palm and fingers.
4. Pay attention to how your body responds to the sensation.
5. Take a few slow breaths while maintaining contact.

MAKE IT YOURS

- Try cool water on your wrists or the back of your neck for a stronger effect.
- Hold something warm against your chest or belly for comfort.
- Alternate between cool and warm if you're feeling really stuck.

Sky Gazing

Looking up at the sky shifts your physical posture and perspective, literally and metaphorically. The vastness of the sky can help put your immediate stress in context, while connecting with nature (even through a window) helps regulate your nervous system through co-regulation with the natural world. Just 30 seconds works if that's all the time you have.

Use When: You feel confined, overwhelmed by small details, or need a sense of perspective.

1. Step outside or look out a window where you can see the sky.
2. Look up and let your gaze soften as you take in the expanse above you.
3. Notice the colors, clouds, light, or stars depending on the time of day.
4. Take three to five slow breaths while keeping your eyes on the sky.
5. Let yourself feel small in a good way, held by something much larger.

MAKE IT YOURS

- Try this at different times of day to notice how the sky changes.
- Lie down on the ground, if possible, to fully immerse in the view.
- Combine with naming what you see (e.g., blue sky, clouds, birds, or planes). Naming this activates your prefrontal cortex and reinforces that you're safe in this moment.

Shake It Out

Shaking is one of the body's natural ways to discharge stress and complete the stress cycle. Animals shake after escaping danger to release trapped activation energy. This practice mimics that instinctive response, helping your nervous system reset and return to regulation.

Use When: You feel tense, stuck, or like energy is trapped in your body.

1. Stand with your feet hip-width apart and knees slightly bent.
2. Start shaking your hands and arms gently, like you're shaking off water.
3. Let the shaking spread through your whole body—shoulders, legs, hips, whatever wants to move.
4. Add sound such as sighs, groans, or just breathing if it feels good.
5. Keep shaking for 30 to 60 seconds, then pause and notice how your body feels.

MAKE IT YOURS

- Start small with just your hands if full-body shaking feels like too much.
- Make it bigger and more vigorous if you need to release more energy.
- Shake for longer if your body wants to keep going.

Acupressure Heart Hold

This acupressure position activates calming points in your hands while the pressure over your heart signals safety to your nervous system. The specific hand hold creates a grounding connection, and holding it at your heart's center mimics the comfort of being held, providing self-soothing through touch.

Use When: You need comfort, feel alone, or want to signal safety to your nervous system.

1. Place your right thumb in the center of your left palm.
2. Wrap your left thumb around your right thumb.
3. Cup your right hand over your left hand, creating a gentle hold.
4. Bring both hands to rest over your heart.
5. Close your eyes, if comfortable, and take slow breaths for 1 to 2 minutes, feeling the warmth and pressure.

MAKE IT YOURS

- If the hand position feels complicated, simply place both palms flat over your heart.
- Try it lying down for deeper relaxation.
- Add a gentle phrase like "I'm here" or "I've got you" if words feel supportive.

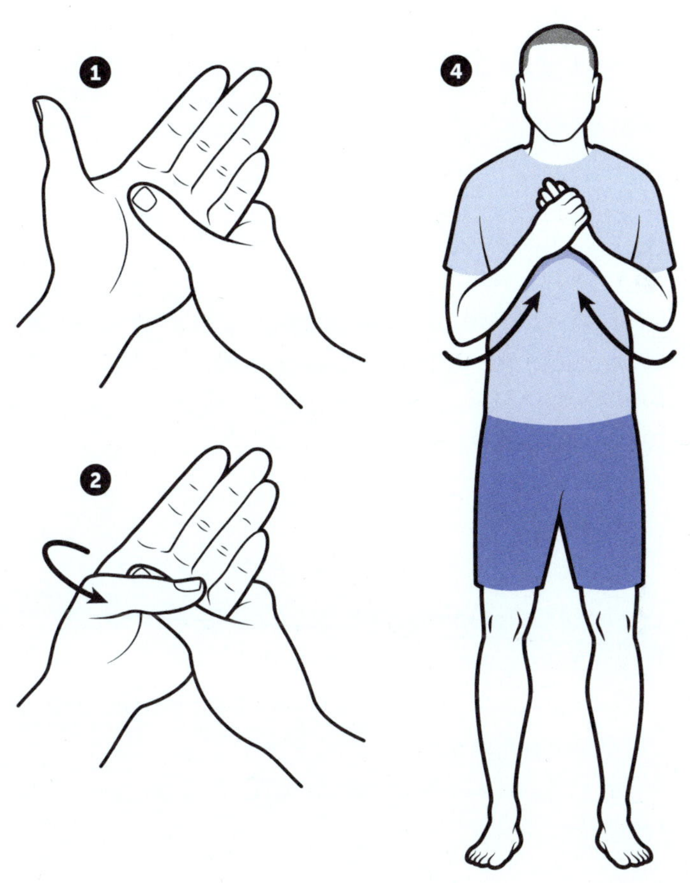
1
2
4

Cold Splash

Cold water on your face triggers the dive reflex, which immediately slows your heart rate and shifts your nervous system state. This physiological response is automatic and can interrupt panic, intense emotion, or dissociation by bringing you back into your body through immediate sensory input.

Use When: You need an immediate reset, feel disconnected, or want to shift out of intense emotion quickly. Try this before bed if racing thoughts are keeping you awake.

1. Run cold water from the tap.
2. Cup your hands and splash cold water on your face, especially your forehead and cheeks.
3. Repeat 2 to 3 times, taking slow breaths between splashes.
4. Pat your face dry and notice how your body feels different.

MAKE IT YOURS

- Use cool water instead of cold if extreme temperature feels too intense.
- Focus the water on your cheeks and forehead where the effect is strongest.
- Follow with a warm towel afterward if you need comfort.

Extended Exhale

Extending your exhale activates the parasympathetic nervous system (your rest and digest mode) and stimulates the vagus nerve. A longer exhale tells your body it's safe to relax, naturally slowing your heart rate and bringing you out of fight-or-flight activation. It's okay to start small—even one extra count on your exhale makes a difference.

Use When: You need to calm down quickly, feel your heart racing, or want to shift from activation to rest.

1. Sit or stand comfortably, letting your shoulders lower a bit.
2. Take a normal breath and count how long your natural inhale and exhale are.
3. On your next breath, keep your inhale the same but extend your exhale by 1 to 2 counts.
4. Pause naturally before your next inhale.
5. Continue for 5 to 10 breaths, keeping your exhale longer than your inhale.

MAKE IT YOURS

- Make an audible sigh on the exhale if that feels releasing.
- Do this lying down if you're trying to sleep or deeply rest.
- Don't force it. If extending feels strained, return to your natural breath.

CHAPTER 4

When You're Shutdown or Frozen

If you've landed here, first of all: I see you. This is a very hard place to be—not because you're doing something wrong, but because shutdown cuts you off from the very resources you'd normally use to help yourself. The fact that you're even looking at this page means something in you is ready to try, and that matters more than you might realize right now.

You might be feeling disconnected, numb, heavy, withdrawn, or spacey. Maybe hopeless. Maybe like you're watching life happening from behind glass as if nothing feels real—you can see it, but you can't quite reach it or feel part of it.

Here's what's happening: Your nervous system has shifted into what's called dorsal vagal shutdown. Think of it as your body's emergency conservation mode. When threat feels inescapable, or when you've been activated for so long that your system simply can't sustain it anymore, your body hits the brakes. It slows everything down, disconnects you from input that feels overwhelming (which, at this point, is practically everything), and goes into protection mode.

This is actually your body doing something incredibly intelligent, even though it doesn't feel good. Shutdown is protection. But the challenge is that when you're here, everything feels harder—from moving and thinking to connecting and caring. It's like wading through mud or like there's a thick fog between you and the world.

So, we're not going to try to jolt you out of this. That's not how it works, and it's not what your system needs. Instead, the practices in this chapter are designed to gently help you come back online at your own pace through small movements, gentle sensations, and rhythmic inputs that quietly signal to your nervous system that it's safe to be here now.

Palming

Rubbing your hands activates your muscles and creates tactile sensation, engaging your senses and bringing you back into your body. The self-generated warmth combined with the gentle pressure of placing your palms over your eyes signals safety to your nervous system. Darkness and heat together are deeply soothing. When you're in shutdown, this practice uses your own body to create comfort without requiring anything external.

Use When: You feel numb, disconnected, or like you can't feel anything.

1. Rub your palms together briskly for 10 to 15 seconds until they feel warm.
2. Cup your warm hands gently over your closed eyes if it feels safe for you.
3. Let the warmth and darkness settle you.
4. Take a few slow breaths, feeling the heat from your palms.
5. Stay here for 30 to 60 seconds, or as long as it feels good.
6. Whisper, "I'm here, I'm coming back."

MAKE IT YOURS

- Rub your hands longer if they don't feel warm enough yet.
- Add gentle pressure over your eyes with your palms if that feels comforting.
- Keep your hands there as long as your body wants the warmth.

Gentle Rocking

Rocking is one of the most primal soothing mechanisms humans have. The rhythmic movement activates your vestibular system (balance and spatial orientation), which helps regulate your nervous system. Rhythm signals predictability and safety. When you're in shutdown, this gentle, repetitive motion can help bring you back online without demanding too much energy.

Use When: You feel frozen, heavy, or like you can't move.

1. Sit or stand comfortably, or lie on your side.
2. Begin rocking gently forward and back or side to side, whichever feels natural.
3. Find a rhythm that feels soothing, like a slow pendulum.
4. Let your body lead; there's no right speed or range of motion.
5. Continue for 1 to 2 minutes, or as long as your body wants to.

MAKE IT YOURS

- Try rocking while hugging a pillow or stuffed animal for added comfort.
- Make the movement smaller if big movements feel like too much.
- Add humming or gentle sounds if that feels good.

Cold Water Sip

Cold water provides immediate sensory input that cuts through the fog of shutdown. Noticing the act of swallowing brings awareness to your internal sensations (interoception), reconnecting you with your body's functions. The deliberate attention to each sip gives your nervous system something concrete to focus on, gently pulling you back into the present moment.

Use When: You feel spacey, foggy, or disconnected from your body.

1. Get a glass or bottle of cold water.
2. Take a small sip and hold it in your mouth for a moment.
3. Notice the temperature and the feeling of the water on your tongue.
4. Swallow slowly and deliberately, feeling the water move down your throat.
5. Take three to five more sips this way, paying attention to each one. (Take more sips if your body would like to continue.)

MAKE IT YOURS

- Try ice water for a stronger sensation if you need more activation.
- Add lemon or mint for an additional sensory element.
- Hold the cold glass in your hands first to feel the temperature.

Rhythmic Drumming

Rhythm organizes the nervous system and provides predictability, which signals safety. The repetitive tapping on a solid surface creates both sound and physical sensation, engaging multiple senses at once. When you're in shutdown, external rhythm can help jump-start your internal rhythms—heartbeat, breathing, and movement—without overwhelming you.

Use When: You feel stuck, flat, or like nothing is moving inside you.

1. Find something solid to drum on, such as a table, countertop, wall, or book.
2. Start tapping out a slow, steady rhythm with your hands or fingertips, like a heartbeat.
3. Keep the beat simple and consistent: tap, tap, tap, tap.
4. Let your body feel the vibration and hear the sound echo.
5. Continue for 1 to 2 minutes, letting the rhythm settle into you.

MAKE IT YOURS

- Speed up slightly if you need more activation; slow down if you need more calm.
- Tap with your knuckles, palms, or fingertips for different sensations.
- Once the basic rhythm feels comfortable, add variety by tapping different patterns or even a favorite song.

Texture Touch

Touch is one of the most direct ways to bring yourself back into your body. When you're in shutdown, your sensory awareness gets muted. Deliberately engaging with texture wakes up the nerve endings in your hands and gives your brain concrete sensory information to process, pulling you back into the present moment.

Use When: You feel numb, like you're behind glass, or can't sense your surroundings.

1. Find something with a noticeable texture nearby, such as a soft blanket, a rough wall, a smooth phone screen, or a fuzzy sweater.
2. Run your fingers slowly across the surface.
3. Notice everything about how it feels: rough, smooth, warm, cool, soft, hard, etc.
4. Press into it, then touch it lightly. See what you notice.
5. Spend 30 to 60 seconds really exploring the texture with your hands.

MAKE IT YOURS

- Try multiple textures one after another for more sensory input.
- Use objects that are already near you so you don't have to get up.
- Touch the texture with different parts of your body, such as your cheek, arm, or foot.
- Close your eyes if that feels comfortable to focus more fully on the sensation.
- Return to a texture that feels particularly grounding whenever you need it.

Ankle Circles

Ankle circles require minimal energy but create movement in your body, which helps bring you out of the frozen immobility of shutdown. The circular motion activates proprioceptive awareness (knowing where your body is in space) and gently wakes up your nervous system without demanding too much. Starting with small, peripheral movements makes activation feel more manageable. This isn't about speed; it's about noticing movement.

Use When: You feel heavy, stuck, or like your body won't move.

1. Sit in a comfortable position.
2. Lift one foot slightly off the ground.
3. Slowly rotate your ankle in a circle in one direction for 5 to 10 rotations.
4. Switch directions and circle the other way 5 to 10 times.
5. Repeat with your other ankle.

MAKE IT YOURS

- Make the circles as small or large as feels comfortable.
- Rest your foot on the ground and just rock it side to side if lifting feels like too much.
- Add wrist circles at the same time if you want more movement.

Scent Snapback

Scent connects directly to the limbic system in your brain, which processes emotion and memory. This makes smell one of the fastest ways to shift your state. When you're in shutdown, a strong or familiar scent can cut through the fog and bring you back to the present moment, activating your senses without requiring physical movement.

Use When: You feel disconnected, foggy, or like you're not really here.

1. Find something with a noticeable scent nearby, such as coffee, a citrus peel, essential oil, mint, hand lotion, or a candle.
2. Bring it close to your nose and take a slow, deliberate inhale.
3. Notice the scent fully. Is it sharp, sweet, earthy, familiar?
4. Take three to five breaths with the scent, letting it fill your awareness.
5. Notice if anything shifts in your body or mind.

MAKE IT YOURS

- Return to the same scent repeatedly to create an anchor for regulation.
- Try different scents to see what works best (e.g., citrus for alertness, lavender for calm, or peppermint for clarity).
- Combine with slow breathing to deepen the sensory experience.

Texture Walk

The soles of your feet have thousands of nerve endings that provide rich sensory information to your brain. Walking barefoot wakes up these receptors and grounds you, literally and neurologically. When you're in shutdown, this combination of gentle movement and strong sensory input helps reconnect you to your body and environment without overwhelming you.

Use When: You can move but feel disconnected from your body or the ground beneath you.

1. Take off your shoes and socks, if possible.
2. Walk slowly across different surfaces, such as carpet, tile, wood floor, grass, or concrete.
3. Notice how each surface feels under your feet, including the temperature, texture, and firmness.
4. Take 5 to 10 steps on each surface, paying full attention to the sensations.
5. Let your feet really feel what they're touching with each step.

MAKE IT YOURS

- Start with just one or two surfaces if multiple surfaces feel like too much.
- Try this outside on grass, dirt, or sand if weather and space allow.
- Go very slowly, taking time to notice each footfall.

Head Rolls

Your neck muscles are innervated by cranial nerves, and your brainstem sits right at the base of your skull. Moving your head gently activates these neural pathways and releases physical tension held in this critical area. When you're in shutdown and your body has been bracing or collapsed, slow head rolls create rhythmic movement that signals safety while directly engaging your nervous system through these important connections. Remember: This isn't about stretching hard; it's about noticing movement.

Use When: You feel tension in your neck, disconnected from your upper body, or stuck in one position.

1. Sit or stand comfortably, letting your shoulders lower a bit.
2. Slowly drop your chin toward your chest, feeling the stretch in the back of your neck.
3. Gently roll your head to one side, bringing your ear toward your shoulder.
4. Continue rolling slowly to the back, then to the other side, and back to center.
5. Repeat 3 to 5 times in each direction, moving as slowly as feels good.

MAKE IT YOURS

- Go side to side if the full rotation feels uncomfortable or makes you dizzy.
- Pause anywhere that feels tight and breathe into that spot.
- Do this lying down if sitting feels like too much.

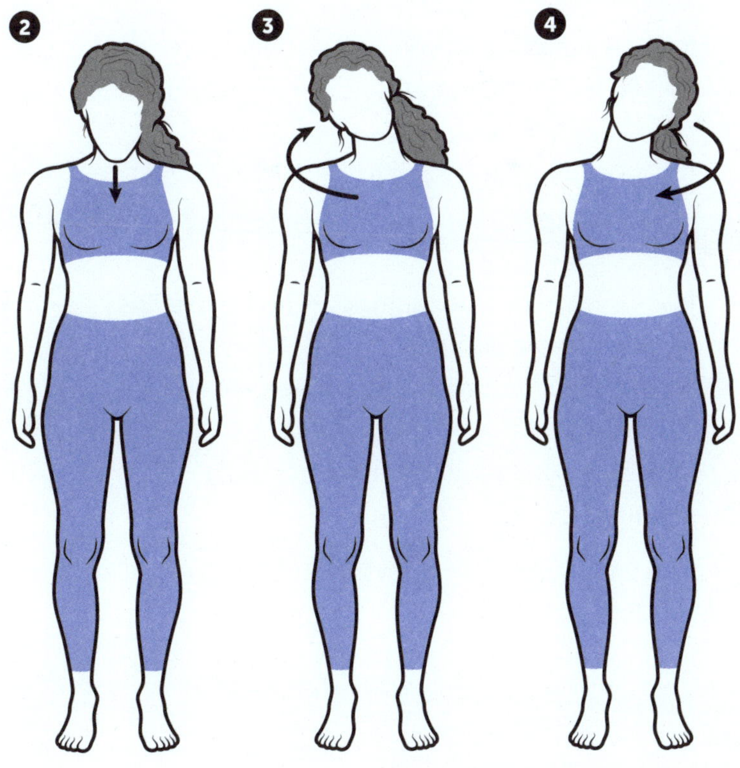

Humming

Humming creates vibration that stimulates the vagus nerve, one of the main pathways for nervous system regulation. The sustained sound requires gentle engagement of your breath and voice, which helps activate your system without demanding too much energy. When you're in shutdown, these internal vibrations can help wake up your body from the inside out.

Use When: You feel flat, empty, or like there's no energy in your body.

1. Sit or lie comfortably, letting your jaw relax slightly.
2. Take a gentle breath in through your nose.
3. As you exhale, hum at whatever pitch feels natural, like "mmmmm."
4. Feel the vibration in your chest, throat, and/or face.
5. Repeat for 5 to 10 breaths, humming through each exhale as long as you can.

MAKE IT YOURS

- Place a hand on your chest or throat to feel the vibration more strongly.
- Hum a familiar tune if a single tone feels boring or hard to sustain.
- Combine with gentle rocking for added soothing rhythm.

Stand and Sway

Standing activates more of your body than sitting or lying down, and the gentle swaying motion engages your vestibular system (balance and spatial awareness), which helps regulate your nervous system. The rhythmic side-to-side movement is naturally soothing. When you're in shutdown, this combination of upright posture and gentle motion helps bring energy back into your body without demanding intensity.

Use When: You've been sitting or lying down for a while and feel stuck or stagnant.

1. Stand with your feet hip-width apart, knees slightly bent.
2. Begin swaying gently side to side, like a tree in a breeze.
3. Let your arms hang loosely or wrap them around yourself.
4. Find a natural rhythm, shifting your weight from one foot to the other.
5. Continue for 1 to 2 minutes, letting the movement be small and easy.

MAKE IT YOURS

- Make the sway smaller if big movements feel like too much.
- Try swaying forward and back instead of side to side.
- Add gentle humming or breathing sounds with the movement.

Upper Body Release

Unlike most muscles in your body, your trapezius is connected directly to your brain through cranial nerves rather than spinal nerves. This direct connection to your brainstem means activating these muscles has a powerful effect on your nervous system. The rotational movement engages your upper body bilaterally, bringing energy and awareness back to your torso. When you're frozen, this gentle activation can help your head feel lighter and your posture naturally lift without forcing it.

Use When: You feel collapsed, heavy in your upper body, or stuck in a slumped position.

1. Sit comfortably on a firm surface, like a chair or bench, keeping your face looking forward.
2. Fold and cross your arms with your hands resting lightly on your elbows.
3. First, let your elbows drop and rest just in front of your body. Rotate your shoulders so your elbows move from side to side, arms gliding lightly over your stomach. Do this three times, moving easily without forcing it.
4. Second, lift your elbows to chest level, in front of your heart. Rotate from side to side three times.
5. Third, Raise your elbows as high as comfortably possible. Rotate from side to side three times.

MAKE IT YOURS

- Move slowly and gently; this isn't about force.
- Skip any part that feels uncomfortable and just do the ones that work.
- Do more than three rotations at each level if your body wants more movement.

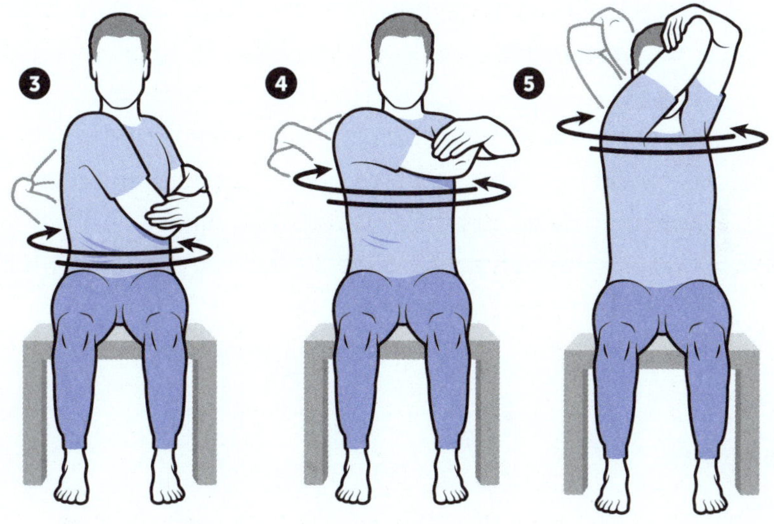

A Living Connection

Your nervous system can co-regulate with other living systems. You might lie with your pet every day or walk past your plants without truly noticing them, but intentionally connecting, really feeling, and paying attention creates a different kind of contact. When you're in shutdown, this deliberate connection with something alive reminds your body that life is still happening, that growth and aliveness exist outside your internal state. This gentle connection can help pull you back into the world without requiring social interaction or complex engagement.

Use When: You feel isolated, disconnected from the world, or like nothing matters.

1. Find something living nearby, such as a houseplant, a pet, a tree outside your window, grass, or even a person, if that feels safe.
2. Place your hand gently on it or hold it.
3. Feel the temperature, texture, and, if possible, any subtle movement (e.g., breathing, leaves rustling).
4. Stay with this contact for 30 to 60 seconds, noticing what it feels like to touch something alive.
5. Take a few slow breaths while maintaining contact.

MAKE IT YOURS

- Use whatever living thing is most accessible; no need to go far.
- If you have a pet, let them rest against you while you notice their breathing.
- Touch a plant's leaves or soil, feeling the life in the texture.

Alternate Hand Squeezes

Alternating hand squeezes create bilateral stimulation that helps integrate the left and right hemispheres of your brain. The rhythmic squeezing gives your body something simple and predictable to focus on, while the proprioceptive feedback (feeling your muscles engage) brings awareness back into your body. When you're in shutdown, this gentle, repetitive action can help activate your system without overwhelming you.

Use When: You feel disconnected from your body or need gentle bilateral activation.

1. Hold something soft in each hand, such as stress balls, rolled socks, or small pillows, or just make fists.
2. Squeeze your right hand, then release.
3. Squeeze your left hand, then release.
4. Continue alternating in a slow, steady rhythm: right, left, right, left.
5. Repeat for 1 to 2 minutes, noticing the sensation in your hands and arms.

MAKE IT YOURS

- Speed up or slow down the rhythm to match what your body needs.
- Try squeezing both hands at the same time instead of alternating.
- Use objects with different textures or densities to vary the sensory input.

Toe Activation

When you're in deep shutdown, even small movements can feel impossible. Starting with your toes, the farthest point from your core, makes movement feel less overwhelming. This distal activation (movement in your extremities) can gently wake up your nervous system without demanding that your whole body engage. Sometimes the smallest movement is the doorway back into your body.

Use When: You feel completely stuck, frozen, or like you can't move at all.

1. Sit, stand, or lie down; whatever position you're already in is fine.
2. Without moving anything else, wiggle your toes.
3. Wiggle them all at once, or one foot at a time, whatever feels easiest.
4. Notice the small movement, the sensation in your toes and feet. This small movement matters.
5. Continue for 30 to 60 seconds, letting this tiny movement be enough.

MAKE IT YOURS

- Try flexing and pointing your feet if wiggling feels awkward.
- If you feel self-conscious, do this under a blanket where no one can see.
- Add ankle circles once toe wiggling feels easy.

CHAPTER 5

When You Feel "Off" or Unclear

You know that feeling when someone asks, "How are you?" and you genuinely have no idea how to answer? Not fine, not terrible, just . . . something. That's where this chapter lives.

If you're here, you might be feeling scattered, meh, stuck, unfocused—like something's not quite right but you can't put your finger on it. Maybe you're restless but tired at the same time. Disconnected but not fully shutdown. It's that in-between space where nothing is clearly wrong, but nothing feels right either.

Here's what's probably happening: Your nervous system is in a mixed state, blending dorsal shutdown with sympathetic activation and creating this fuzzy, unclear experience. Part of you wants to collapse, part of you wants to run, and the result is that you just feel . . . weird. It's like your internal GPS is buffering—you're not frozen and you're not flooded; you're just stuck somewhere in the middle doing a little bit of everything and none of it particularly well.

This can actually be one of the most frustrating places to be because there's no clear signal telling you what you need. When you're activated, you know you need to calm down. When you're shutdown, you know you need to come back online. But when you're just *off*? It's harder to know where to start.

The practices in this chapter are designed to cut through the fog. They help you reorient, reconnect, and build clarity—giving your nervous system something concrete to do so it can stop spinning its wheels. Think of these as your reset-and-reassess tools. Sometimes you just need to move the energy, shift your focus, or give your body a clear task so you can figure out where you are and what you actually need.

Bilateral Eye Tracking

Bilateral eye movements help integrate the left and right hemispheres of your brain, which can feel disconnected when you're in that off state. This gentle tracking gives your brain a clear task and can help organize scattered thoughts. The side-to-side motion is similar to what happens during REM sleep when your brain processes information.

Use When: You feel foggy, scattered, or like your thoughts won't organize.

1. Sit or lie comfortably, keeping your head still.
2. Without moving your head, slowly look all the way to the right with just your eyes.
3. Pause for a moment, then slowly move your eyes all the way to the left.
4. Continue moving your eyes side to side in a slow, steady rhythm.
5. Repeat 10 to 15 times, or until you notice a shift, such as yawning, sighing, or deeper breathing.

MAKE IT YOURS

- Choose fixed points on each side (such as a photo, a window, a doorframe) to give your eyes clear destinations.
- Follow your finger or a pen if you need something concrete to track.
- Combine with slow breathing, one breath per eye movement.

Crossbody Integration

Crossbody movements integrate the left and right hemispheres of your brain, helping create clarity when your system feels fragmented. Diagonal reaching activates coordination and spatial awareness, giving your nervous system a clear pattern to follow. When you're feeling off, this organized movement can help bring you back to center.

Use When: You feel stuck, disconnected between your left and right side, or need to wake up your body.

1. Stand or sit with your arms relaxed at your sides.
2. Reach your right hand across your body toward your left knee or left side of the room.
3. Return to center, then reach your left hand toward your right knee or right side of the room.
4. Continue alternating, reaching diagonally across your body in a steady rhythm.
5. Do 10 to 15 reaches on each side, letting the movement be fluid and easy.

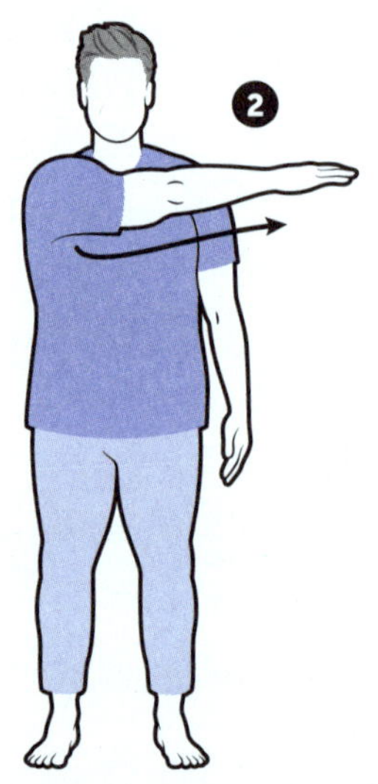

MAKE IT YOURS

- Make the reaches bigger and more dramatic if you need more activation.
- Add a slight twist in your torso for more movement.
- Speed up for more energy; slow down for more control.

Fine-Motor Sequencing

Fine-motor control requires focus and coordination, which helps organize your scattered attention. The sequential pattern gives your brain a clear task to follow, while the repetitive rhythm is naturally regulating. When you're feeling unclear, this simple practice brings you into your body and the present moment through precise, controlled movement.

Use When: You feel restless, unfocused, or need something simple to ground your attention.

1. Rest your hands comfortably on your lap or a table.
2. Tap each finger to your thumb in sequence: pointer, middle, ring, and pinky.
3. Do this on both hands at the same time, moving through the pattern.
4. Repeat the sequence 5 to 10 times, keeping a steady rhythm.
5. Notice the sensation of each finger touching your thumb.

MAKE IT YOURS

- Try one hand at a time if doing both feels too complicated.
- Reverse the order (pinky to pointer) once the forward pattern feels easy.
- Add counting out loud as you tap each finger.

Downregulate with Counting

Counting backward requires just enough mental effort to interrupt scattered thoughts without being overwhelming. Speaking out loud engages your voice, breath, and hearing simultaneously, bringing multiple senses online. When you're feeling off, this clear, structured task gives your brain something concrete to do, which helps organize your internal experience.

Use When: Your mind is spinning in circles, you can't focus, or you need a clear mental task.

1. Pick a starting number between 10 and 20.
2. Say the number out loud, then count backward: "Fifteen . . . fourteen . . . thirteen . . ."
3. Continue all the way down to zero, speaking each number clearly.
4. If you lose track, start over from your chosen number.
5. Notice how your mind feels after completing the countdown.

MAKE IT YOURS

- Start with a lower number (like 10) if backward counting feels hard.
- Count faster if you need more activation, slower if you need more calm.
- Whisper if you're in public, or count in your head as a last resort.

Perimeter Scan

Following visual boundaries helps organize your spatial awareness and reorients you in your environment. When you're feeling off, your sense of where you are can get fuzzy. This practice grounds you by giving your visual system a clear path to follow, helping your brain map the space around you and remember that you exist in a specific place.

Use When: You feel disoriented, spacey, or disconnected from your surroundings.

1. From wherever you're sitting or standing, look up at where the wall meets the ceiling.
2. Slowly trace this line with your eyes, following it all the way around the room as far as you can from your position. It's fine if you can't see it all from where you are.
3. Keep your head still and let just your eyes do the moving.
4. Notice corners, angles, and changes in direction as you follow the edge.
5. Complete the perimeter as best you can.

MAKE IT YOURS

- Try tracing doorframes, windows, or furniture edges if ceiling lines feel too high.
- Trace the same line multiple times if once doesn't feel like enough.
- Go slower if you feel dizzy or disoriented.

Resistance Press

Pressing against resistance activates your muscles and proprioceptive system, bringing awareness and energy into your body. The isometric pressure (pushing without movement) grounds you physically while giving your nervous system clear feedback about your strength and boundaries. When you're feeling off, this solid, contained effort can help you feel more present and defined.

Use When: You feel stuck, passive, or like you need to activate your body.

1. Stand in a doorway with your feet hip-width apart.
2. Place your palms flat on either side of the doorframe at shoulder height.
3. Press outward into the frame as if you're trying to widen the doorway.
4. Hold the press for 5 to 10 seconds, engaging your arms, chest, and core.
5. Release, step back, and notice how your body feels. Repeat 3 to 5 times.

MAKE IT YOURS

- Hold the press longer or shorter depending on what feels right.
- Add an audible exhale or sigh while pressing for more release.
- Use a wall or sturdy counter if no doorway is available.

Catch and Release

Tossing and catching requires hand-eye coordination, visual tracking, and timing, which engage multiple brain regions simultaneously. This pulls you out of mental loops and into physical action. The playful element helps shift your state without feeling like serious effort. When you're feeling off, giving your brain and body a clear, engaging task can cut through the fog. Use whatever soft object is nearby; no special item is needed. Remember, this is about play, not perfection.

Use When: You feel stuck in your head, need to move energy, or want to improve coordination.

1. Find a soft object you can toss, such as a ball, rolled-up socks, a small pillow, or a stuffed animal.
2. Toss it gently from one hand to the other, following it with your eyes.
3. Keep a steady rhythm, letting the toss become automatic.
4. Stay engaged with the movement, catching and tossing.
5. Continue for 1 to 2 minutes, noticing how your focus shifts.

MAKE IT YOURS

- Start with easy, low tosses if coordination feels shaky.
- Toss higher or faster once you feel steady.
- Try it while standing, sitting, or even walking.

Vowel Activation

Each vowel sound creates different vibrations in your body and engages your vocal system in unique ways. Moving through the vowels activates your breath, voice, and nervous system, helping you shift from that stuck off feeling. The variation keeps your attention engaged while the vocalization helps release stagnant energy and brings clarity.

Use When: You feel muted, unclear, or like you can't express what's happening inside.

1. Sit or stand comfortably, letting your jaw relax.
2. Take a breath, and on the exhale, make a long *aaaa* sound.
3. On the next breath, try *eeeee*, then *iiiii*, then *ooooo*, then *uuuuu*.
4. Move through all five vowels, noticing how each one feels and sounds different.
5. Repeat the sequence 2 to 3 times, playing with pitch and volume.

MAKE IT YOURS

- Make some sounds loud and others soft to explore range.
- Place a hand on your chest or throat to feel the vibrations.
- Focus on whichever vowel creates the most sensation in your body.

Grounding Inventory

Combining physical pressure with verbal naming engages both your body awareness and your cognitive processing. The pressure activates proprioceptive receptors that tell your brain where you are in space, while speaking the body part out loud reinforces the connection between your mind and body. When you're feeling off, this dual engagement helps you land back in your physical self.

Use When: You feel disconnected from your body or like you're floating outside yourself.

1. Sit or lie down on a firm surface.
2. Press one part of your body firmly into the surface (e.g., your feet into the floor, your back into the chair, or your hands into your thighs).
3. As you press, say out loud what you're pressing: "I'm pressing my feet into the floor."
4. Move to a different body part, press it down, and name it.
5. Continue for 5 to 7 body parts, pressing and naming each one.

MAKE IT YOURS

- Press harder if you need more sensation or lighter if you need gentleness.
- Whisper the names if speaking out loud feels awkward.
- Notice which body parts feel most present and which feel furthest away.

Mobile Triangle Breath

Triangle breathing (equal counts for inhale, hold, and exhale) creates a balanced rhythm that helps regulate your nervous system. Adding steps requires coordination between breath and movement, which gives your brain a clear pattern to follow and helps integrate scattered energy. When you're feeling off, this structured practice brings clarity through rhythm and purpose.

Use When: You feel unfocused, restless, or like your body and breath are disconnected.

1. Stand comfortably in a spot where you have space to take a few steps forward.
2. Inhale for three counts while taking three steps forward.
3. Hold your breath for three counts while standing still.
4. Exhale for three counts while taking three steps backward.
5. Repeat this cycle 5 to 10 times, coordinating breath with movement.

MAKE IT YOURS

- Try stepping side to side instead of forward and back.
- Do this in place if you don't have room to move.
- Skip the breath hold if that feels uncomfortable, and just alternate inhale/exhale with stepping.

Percussion Reset

Clapping creates immediate sensory input through sound, touch, and vibration. The bilateral hand contact activates both sides of your body and brain simultaneously. The rhythmic repetition is organizing and grounding. When you're feeling off, this simple, sharp sensation can cut through the fog and bring you into the present moment quickly.

Use When: You feel dull, foggy, or need to shift your energy quickly.

1. Stand or sit comfortably with your hands free.
2. Start clapping at a steady pace, loud enough to really hear and feel it.
3. Keep a consistent rhythm, letting the sound and sensation fill your awareness.
4. Continue for 30 to 60 seconds, paying attention to the sound, the sting in your palms, and the rhythm.
5. Stop and notice how your body and mind feel different.

MAKE IT YOURS

- Clap just your fingertips together if full hand claps feel too intense.
- Clap above your head, in front of your chest, or down low for variety.
- Add stomping your feet at the same time for more activation.

Nondominant Switch

Using your nondominant hand interrupts automatic patterns and forces your brain to pay attention. This cognitive challenge pulls you out of the fuzzy off state by requiring focus and coordination. The unfamiliarity creates presence—you can't space out when you're trying to write with your opposite hand. This simple disruption can help reset your system and bring clarity.

Use When: You feel stuck on autopilot, foggy, or like you need to interrupt your usual patterns.

1. Choose a simple task you normally do with your dominant hand, such as stirring coffee, opening a door, brushing your teeth, or writing your name.
2. Do that task with your nondominant hand instead.
3. Go slowly and pay full attention to how awkward and deliberate it feels.
4. Notice the concentration it requires and how present you become.
5. Spend 1 to 2 minutes doing the task, staying curious about the unfamiliar sensation.

MAKE IT YOURS

- Start with very simple tasks like opening a jar or holding a cup if complex ones feel frustrating.
- Try multiple small tasks in a row with your opposite hand.
- Try to laugh at how clumsy it feels rather than striving for control.

Seated Spinal Release

Spinal twists release tension held in your torso and create movement in your core, which can feel locked up when you're in that unclear state. Combining the twist with intentional breathing helps organize your system and creates space internally. The rotation also gently activates your digestive organs and helps shift stagnant energy when you're feeling stuck.

Use When: You feel stagnant, compressed, or like energy is stuck in your torso.

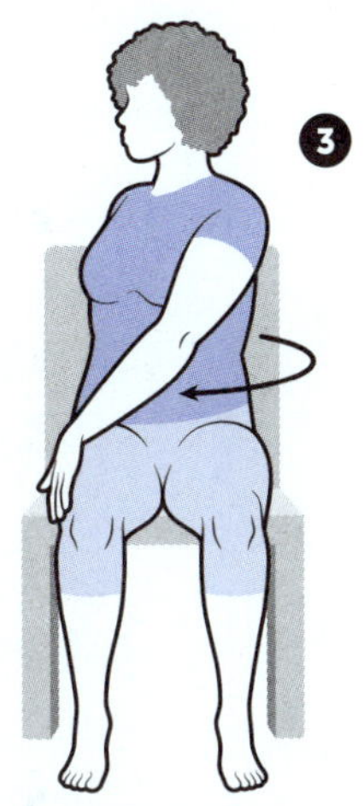

1. Sit upright in a chair with your feet flat on the floor.
2. Inhale and lengthen your spine, sitting up a bit taller.
3. As you exhale, gently twist to the right, placing your left hand on your right knee and your right hand behind you on the chair.
4. Let the gaze follow the twist, looking over your shoulder.
5. Hold the twist for 2 to 3 breaths, feeling the rotation in your spine.
6. Inhale back to center, then exhale and twist to the left. Repeat 3 to 5 times on each side.

MAKE IT YOURS

- Make the twist smaller if deep rotation feels uncomfortable.
- Hold the position longer (for 5 to 6 breaths) if that feels good.
- Try this standing instead of sitting for a fuller range of motion.

Pattern Disruption

Walking backward interrupts your brain's autopilot and forces you to pay complete attention to movement and space. Your body has walked forward millions of times, but walking backward requires conscious effort and coordination. This pattern disruption pulls you out of the foggy off state by demanding presence and focus. The unfamiliarity resets your system.

Use When: You feel stuck on autopilot, trapped in familiar patterns, or need to disrupt your usual way of moving.

1. Find a clear, safe space where you can take several steps backward.
2. Check your surroundings so you can see where you're going.
3. Slowly walk backward for 10 to 15 steps, being deliberate with each foot placement.
4. Notice how much attention and coordination this requires.
5. Walk forward and return to your starting point, then go backward again. Repeat 2 to 3 times.

MAKE IT YOURS

- Hold on to a wall or railing if balance feels uncertain.
- Try it in a hallway where you have clear boundaries.
- Walk sideways if walking backward feels too disorienting.

Facial Expressions

Cranial nerves that connect directly to your brainstem and emotional centers control your facial muscles. Making deliberate expressions activates these pathways and can actually shift your emotional state. When you're feeling off and can't access what you're feeling, moving your face through different expressions helps reconnect you with your emotional range and wakes up your nervous system.

Use When: You feel flat, expressionless, or disconnected from your emotions.

1. Sit or stand in front of a mirror if possible, or just feel your face as you move it.
2. Make an exaggerated surprised face: wide eyes, raised eyebrows, and open mouth. Hold for three seconds.
3. Switch to an angry face: furrowed brow, clenched jaw, and narrowed eyes. Hold for three seconds.
4. Make a disgusted face: wrinkled nose and raised upper lip. Hold for 3 seconds.
5. Make a sad face: downturned mouth and droopy eyes. Hold for 3 seconds.
6. End with a big happy face: huge smile, raised cheeks, and crinkled eyes. Hold for 5 seconds.
7. Take a breath and whisper, "I'm allowed to feel all of this."

MAKE IT YOURS

- Exaggerate each expression for stronger activation.
- Notice which expressions feel harder or more genuine.
- Really hold that final happy face and see if your mood shifts even slightly.

CHAPTER 6

When You Feel Angry or Agitated

So, you're pissed. Or irritable. Or one comment away from losing it completely. Maybe you've already snapped at someone. Welcome—you've come to the right place.

If this describes you right now, you might be feeling rage, a tight jaw, clenched fists, and explosive energy building. Everything feels too much, too loud, too close. You want to either fight something or get the hell out. Maybe both.

Here's what's happening: You're mobilized and charged, ready for action. Know that this isn't bad or wrong. Anger is information and energy. It's often a sign that a boundary has been crossed, that something matters to you, or that you need to protect something important. The problem isn't that you're angry. The problem is that most of us were taught to suppress it, ignore it, or apologize for it—which just leaves all that activation trapped in your system with nowhere to go.

We're not going to try to calm you down or make the anger disappear. That's not how this works, and honestly, that approach has probably failed you before. Instead, the practices in this chapter are about giving your anger somewhere to go so it doesn't stay stuck in your body or explode onto the wrong target. You get to feel it fully and move it through your system safely.

Let's put that energy to work.

Tear-Paper Rage Ritual

This gives your body a safe, symbolic outlet for fight energy. Your nervous system registers action and release without real threat or damage, reducing internal pressure. Expressive rituals like this are especially powerful when paired with self-compassion at the end.

Use When: You feel irritable, angry, or on the edge of snapping.

1. Grab a stack of scrap paper or an old magazine.
2. Set a timer for 90 seconds.
3. Tear the paper slowly, quickly, or loudly—whatever feels good. Add sound if it helps; growl, grunt, or shout.
4. When the timer ends, pause and place your hands on your heart, chest, or belly.
5. Whisper, "I'm allowed to feel."

MAKE IT YOURS

- No paper? Try snapping dry spaghetti, punching a pillow, or stomping your feet.
- Prefer quiet? Use your breath to blow the energy out like wind.
- Add a ritual close: Wash your hands, shake out your arms, or step outside to signal completion.

Stomp and Growl

Stomping grounds the fight energy down through your legs and into the earth, giving it somewhere to go. The impact activates large muscle groups and proprioceptive feedback, bringing awareness back into your body. Adding the growl engages your throat and diaphragm, releasing tension held in your jaw and vocal cords. Together, these create a full-body discharge of aggressive energy in a way that's safe and contained.

Use When: You feel explosive, aggressive, or like you need to get energy out of your body right now.

1. Stand with your feet hip-width apart, knees slightly bent.
2. Stomp one foot down hard into the ground, feeling the impact.
3. As you stomp, let out a growl from deep in your throat.
4. Alternate feet, stomping and growling with each impact.
5. Continue for 30 to 60 seconds, letting the intensity match your anger.

MAKE IT YOURS

- Stomp harder and growl louder if you need more release.
- Try just stomping without sound, or just growling without movement, to see what works best.
- Add arm movements like fists pumping if your upper body wants to join.

Palm Tension Press

Pressing with maximum force activates large muscle groups and gives your fight energy a safe outlet. The isometric contraction (pressing without movement) builds intensity then releases it, helping discharge the activation trapped in your system. Letting your body shake during the press allows natural tremoring and release. This contained expression lets you feel your strength and power without causing harm.

Use When: You feel tension building, your fists are clenched, or you need to contain explosive energy.

1. Bring your palms together in front of your chest, fingers pointing up.
2. Press your palms together as hard as you possibly can, engaging your arms, chest, and core.
3. Hold the press for 5 to 10 seconds, breathing through the intensity. Let yourself shake with the effort.
4. Release completely, letting your arms drop and muscles soften.
5. Repeat 5 to 10 times, or until you feel the charge decrease.

MAKE IT YOURS

- Add a forceful exhale or sound when you release the press.
- Press your fists together instead of palms if that feels more powerful.
- Alternate between pressing and shaking out your arms between rounds.

Lion's Breath

Lion's breath combines forceful exhalation with facial contortion and vocalization, releasing tension held in your jaw, throat, and face. The tongue extension activates the vagus nerve, while the aggressive exhale discharges fight energy. This practice gives you permission to be fierce and expressive in a contained, intentional way.

Use When: You feel rage in your throat or chest, tension in your face, or like you need to roar.

1. Sit or kneel comfortably, hands resting on your knees or thighs.
2. Take a deep breath in through your nose.
3. Open your mouth wide, then stick your tongue out and down toward your chin (yes, you're going to look ridiculous, embrace it).
4. Exhale forcefully with a loud *HAAA* sound, like a lion roaring at someone who really deserves it.
5. Repeat 3 to 5 times, letting the exhale be fierce and satisfying.

MAKE IT YOURS

- Try it on all fours like an actual lion for more embodiment.
- Do it silently if you need to be quiet, but try to keep the facial expression intense.
- Look up toward the sky or ceiling as you exhale for fuller throat extension.

Pillow Scream

Screaming is one of the most direct ways to discharge rage from your system. The pillow muffles the sound so you can be as loud as you need without disturbing others or feeling self-conscious. The forceful vocalization releases tension in your throat, jaw, and diaphragm while giving your fight energy a clear outlet. Your nervous system registers the release even though no one else hears it.

Use When: You feel like you're going to explode, need to yell, or have rage that needs to come out *now*.

1. Grab a pillow and take a deep breath in.
2. Press the pillow firmly against your face, covering your mouth and nose.
3. Scream into the pillow as loud and long as you can on the exhale.
4. Pull the pillow away, take a breath, and repeat.
5. Keep screaming until you feel the intensity decrease, usually 3 to 7 rounds.

MAKE IT YOURS

- Try screaming specific words or sounds that match your anger.
- Add pounding your fists into the bed or couch while you scream.
- Take breaks between screams to notice how your body feels different.

Arm Circles

Fast, large arm movements discharge fight energy through your upper body and shoulders where anger often gets trapped. The momentum and speed give your aggression somewhere to go without harming anything. Focusing on one arm at a time lets you put full intensity into each movement.

Use When: You feel agitated energy in your upper body, restless, or like you need to move fast.

1. Stand with your feet hip-width apart, arms at your sides.
2. Start swinging your right arm in a giant circle: forward, up over your head, back behind you, and around again, like a windmill.
3. Go as fast as you can, making the circles as large and aggressive as possible.
4. After 10 to 15 circles forward, reverse direction and circle backward with the same arm.
5. Switch to your left arm and repeat. Continue alternating for 1 to 2 minutes total.

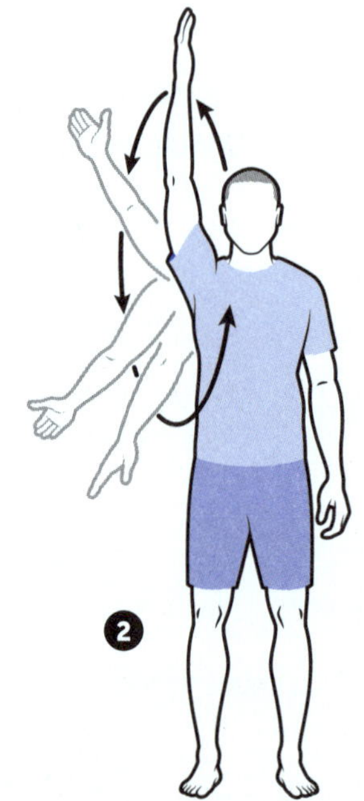

MAKE IT YOURS

- Try both arms simultaneously if single-arm circles aren't enough to express the energy you're feeling.
- Add sounds such as grunts, exhales, and yells with each rotation.
- Do this outside if you have space to really let loose.

Bite Down

Your jaw holds tremendous tension, especially when you're angry. Biting down intentionally with something safe gives you permission to use that jaw strength without causing damage. The compression and release help discharge energy trapped in your temporomandibular joint (the hinge connecting your jaw to your skull) and facial muscles. This can be especially satisfying because we're often told not to clench or grind, but sometimes your body just needs to do it with purpose.

Use When: You feel jaw tension, clenched teeth, or rage locked in your face.

1. Find something safe to bite, such as a rolled towel, silicone cutlery, or oral stimulation fidgets.
2. Place it between your back molars on one side.
3. Bite down hard, as hard as feels good, engaging your jaw muscles fully.
4. Hold for 5 to 10 seconds, then release.
5. Switch sides and repeat. Do 5 to 10 rounds on each side.

MAKE IT YOURS

- Bite harder if you need more intensity or softer if your jaw or teeth are sensitive.
- Try biting down while making a growling sound for added release.
- Massage your jaw muscles with your fingertips after to release any remaining tension.

Crossbody Punches

Crossbody punching combines bilateral movement with safe impact (hitting air), giving your fight response a clear outlet. The alternating motion integrates left and right hemispheres while the forceful movement discharges rage through your arms, shoulders, and core. Your nervous system gets to complete the fight impulse without actually fighting anyone.

Use When: You feel aggressive, combative, or like you need to hit something (safely).

1. Stand with your feet hip-width apart, fists up near your chest.
2. Keep your core tight, and punch your right fist across your body toward the left, as if hitting an imaginary target in front of you.
3. Return to center, then punch your left fist across toward the right.
4. Continue alternating punches in a steady rhythm, letting them be fast and forceful.
5. Keep going for 30 to 60 seconds, or until the aggressive energy decreases.

MAKE IT YOURS

- Add a shout or grunt with each punch for vocal release.
- Try punching straight ahead instead of across your body if that feels better.
- Imagine punching through the thing that's making you angry (symbolically).

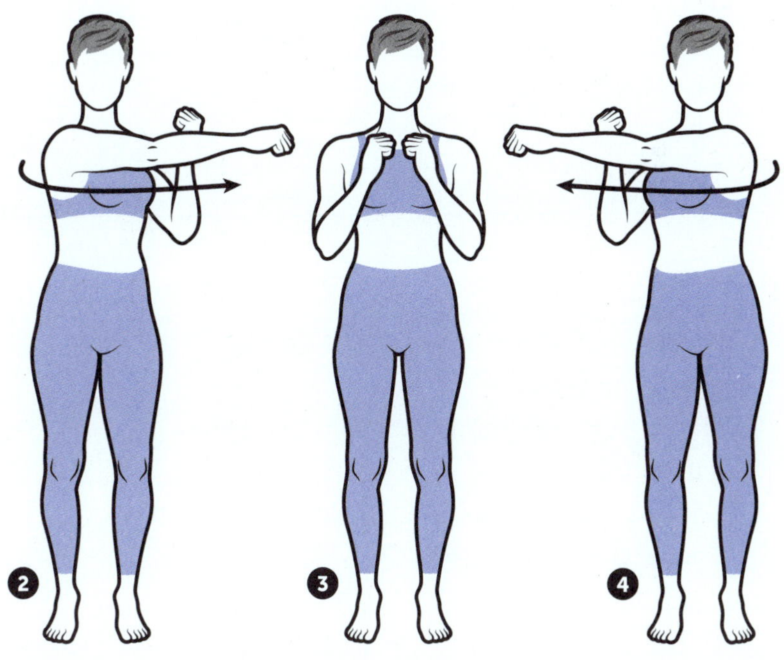

Whisper Then Shout

Building from whisper to shout gives you a safe container to practice intensity and expression. Starting quiet helps you stay in control while the progression gives your anger permission to crescendo. Your nervous system gets to experience the full range from containment to release, which can be more satisfying than just exploding. The contrast helps you feel your power while staying connected to choice.

Use When: You feel rage building, need to express something, or want to practice intensity without losing control.

1. Choose a word or short phrase such as "no," "stop," "enough," or whatever fits your anger. If these words feel too loaded, try "out," "move," "go," or even just a sound like "ahhh."
2. Whisper it quietly, feeling the restraint.
3. Say it at a normal volume.
4. Say it louder.
5. Shout it as loud as you can, letting the full force come out.

MAKE IT YOURS

- Try different words to see which ones carry the most charge for you.
- Skip straight to shouting if building up feels frustrating.
- Reverse it afterward (shout to whisper) to help bring your system back down.

Pillow Punch

Punching a pillow or cushion provides actual impact and contact, which your fight response is craving. The soft surface absorbs the force safely, letting you be as aggressive as you need without hurting yourself or anything else. The repetitive striking motion discharges rage through your arms and core while your nervous system gets to complete the impulse to fight back.

Use When: You feel physically aggressive, need impact, or want to hit something without consequences.

1. Grab a pillow or cushion and place it on your bed, couch, or floor.
2. Make fists and stand or kneel in front of it.
3. Punch the pillow repeatedly with alternating fists, as hard as you want.
4. Let yourself be aggressive: fast punches; slow, heavy ones; or whatever your body needs.
5. Continue for 30 to 60 seconds, or until you feel the charge shift.

MAKE IT YOURS

- Punch harder if you need more force, or use lighter jabs if full force feels too intense.
- Shout, grunt, or yell with each punch for more release.
- Stack multiple pillows for a bigger target, or use your mattress.

Complete the Defense Response

The push-away motion completes a defensive response your body wants to make when boundaries are violated or threats are too close. Anger often arises when something has crossed a line, and your nervous system needs to restore distance and safety. This movement gives your fight response a clear action to complete, discharging the energy while reinforcing your right to create space.

Use When: You feel invaded, violated, or like you need to create distance from something or someone.

1. Stand with your feet firmly planted, arms bent with hands at chest level.
2. Forcefully extend both arms straight out in front of you, palms facing forward, as if shoving something away. You can step one foot forward to keep your balance if needed.
3. Pull your arms back to your chest and immediately push away again.
4. Repeat in a steady rhythm, letting each push be strong and decisive.
5. Continue for 30 to 60 seconds, or 15 to 20 pushes, making each one count.

MAKE IT YOURS

- Say "No" or "Get away" or "Stop" with each push for added power.
- Try pushing to the sides or overhead if forward doesn't feel right.
- Alternate between big, forceful pushes and quicker, repeated ones.

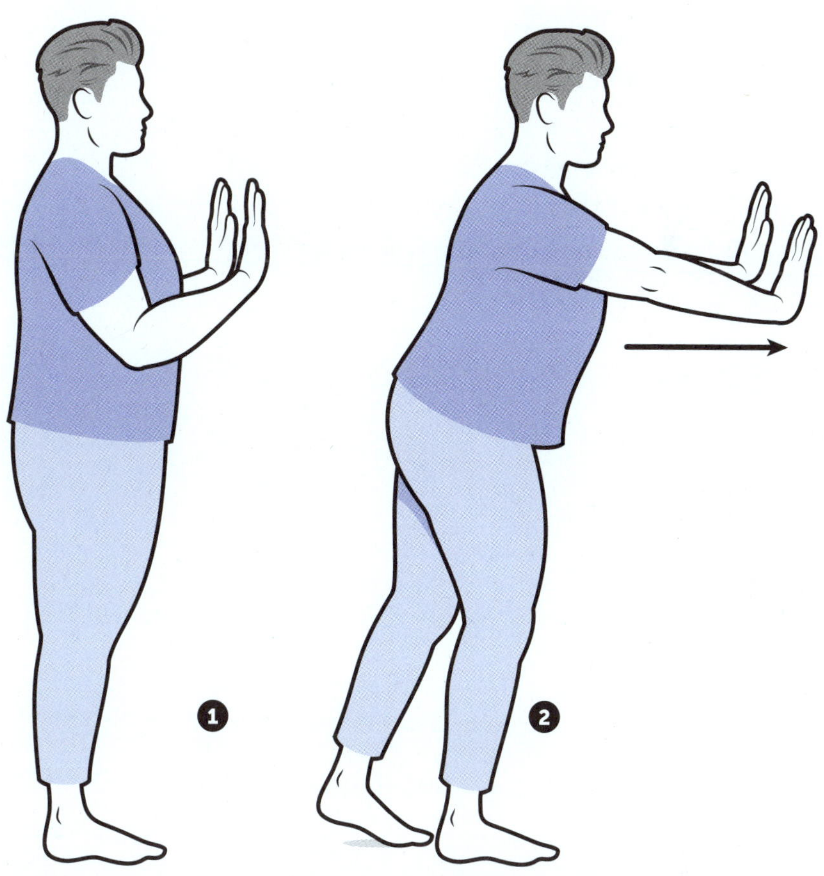

Forceful "HA"

Forceful "HA" breathing combines sharp exhalation with full-body movement, creating an explosive release of energy. The diaphragmatic engagement and vocalization discharge tension from your core and throat. This martial arts–inspired technique gives fight energy a powerful, controlled outlet while repetition helps complete the stress cycle. Each "HA" is a small, contained explosion that adds up to significant discharge.

Use When: You feel explosive energy, need sharp release, or want to feel energized.

1. Stand with your feet hip-width apart, knees slightly bent.
2. Raise your arms overhead.
3. Take a quick breath in, then forcefully swing your arms down while bending your knees.
4. As your arms come down, exhale sharply with a loud "HA!" from your belly.
5. Repeat 10 to 20 times in quick succession, letting the movement and sound be explosive.

MAKE IT YOURS

- Go faster for more intensity or slower for more control.
- Try it without the arm movement if you're in a small space.
- Make the "HA" louder or add variations like "HEY" or "HOO."
- Do fewer reps if you feel lightheaded, building up over time.
- Follow with a few slow breaths to help your system settle after the intensity.

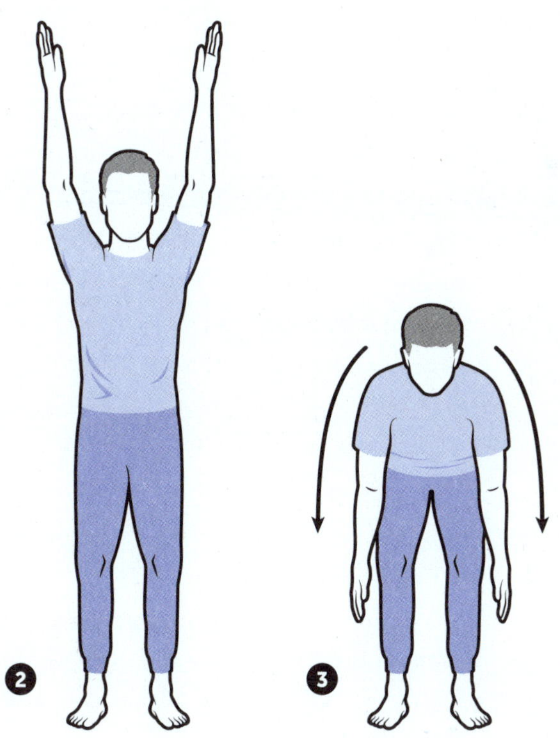

Name What You're Protecting

Anger is almost always protective; it shows up when something you care about is threatened. Naming what you're protecting helps you understand your anger as information rather than just destructive energy. This cognitive reframe doesn't make the anger disappear, but it helps you see it as a reasonable response to a real need, which can reduce shame and help you respond more effectively.

Use When: You feel defensive, reactive, or stuck in anger and need perspective.

1. Pause in the middle of your anger and ask yourself, "What am I protecting right now?" This may be your time, your boundaries, your safety, your values, someone you love, or something else.
2. Say it out loud or write it down.
3. Acknowledge that this anger is here because something matters to you.
4. Take a breath and feel the difference between "I'm angry" and "I'm protecting something important."
5. Notice if naming what you're protecting changes the intensity or quality of your anger.
6. Let this awareness shift how you hold the anger.

MAKE IT YOURS

- Write out a full list of everything you're protecting if one thing isn't enough.
- Use this before or after you discharge anger physically, whenever it feels right.
- Return to this practice when anger feels confusing or out of proportion.

Silent Scream

Silent screaming gives you the facial and throat activation of screaming without the sound, making it accessible anywhere. The intense facial contortion activates cranial nerves and releases tension held in your jaw, throat, and face. Your body still registers the effort and expression even without vocalization. This can be especially useful when you're in public, at work, or anywhere you need to discharge rage quietly.

Use When: You feel rage but can't act on it yet, or you want to scream but need to do so quietly.

1. Sit or stand wherever you are.
2. Open your mouth as wide as possible, like you're screaming.
3. Engage all your facial muscles: Scrunch or widen your eyes, furrow your brow, and tense your jaw. If your face (or body) trembles or shakes, let it. That's discharge happening.
4. Push air out forcefully but silently, feeling your throat and face contract.
5. Hold for 5 to 10 seconds, then release. Repeat 5 to 10 times.
6. When you're done, place a hand on your chest and whisper, "This rage is information, not failure."

MAKE IT YOURS

- Try it alone in a place where you can be as dramatic as you want.
- Alternate between silent and audible screams to explore the difference.
- Massage your jaw and face afterward if they feel tight.

Intentional Tremor

Tensing your entire body so intensely that it shakes creates maximum engagement of your musculature and nervous system. The tremoring that happens during peak tension is your body's natural way of discharging stuck energy. This allows rage to move through your system rather than staying trapped. The full-body nature of this practice matches the all-consuming feeling of intense anger.

Use When: You feel rage throughout your entire body and need a full-body discharge.

1. Stand with your feet hip-width apart.
2. Tense every muscle in your body at once: Clench your fists, tighten your core, squeeze your legs, and scrunch your face.
3. Keep squeezing harder and harder until your body starts to shake from the intensity of the tension.
4. Hold this shaking tension for 3 to 10 seconds, letting your body tremble with the effort.
5. Release everything at once and let your arms drop. Repeat 3 to 5 times.
6. After your final release, take a breath and say, "I'm allowed to feel this angry."
7. Follow with gentle stretching or shaking out to help your muscles recover.

MAKE IT YOURS

- Squeeze even harder if you're not shaking yet.
- Add sounds such as growling or grunting while you're in the tension.
- Try it lying down if standing feels unstable.

CHAPTER 7

When You're Anxious or Overwhelmed

Your heart is racing, your thoughts won't stop, and you feel like you might jump out of your own skin. Everything feels urgent and nothing feels manageable. Also, did you remember to send that email? And why is your chest so tight?

If this is where you are right now, you're not losing your mind—your nervous system is in sympathetic overdrive with a flight tone. You're activated and mobilized, but instead of fighting, your system wants to escape. The problem is that most modern stressors aren't things you can literally run from—your inbox, that difficult conversation, your own brain at 3 a.m.—so all that escape energy gets trapped in your body with nowhere to go.

You might be feeling jittery, tight-chested, easily startled, and like you're spiraling. Your body is buzzing with energy, but it's not the productive kind. It's the "I might spontaneously combust in the middle of this grocery store" kind. You want to run but there's nowhere to go, so instead you're just vibrating in place.

Here's the thing: Your body is doing exactly what it's designed to do. It sensed something that needed your attention and flooded you with the energy to escape. That's not a malfunction. But when there's no actual bear to run from, that energy needs somewhere to go.

We're not going to try to force you to calm down—that never works anyway. Instead, the practices in this chapter help downshift your activation by giving your nervous system clear evidence that you're not actually being chased: small, grounding, steady signals that say you're safe, you can settle, and the emergency is over.

Let's bring you back down to earth.

5-4-3-2-1 Grounding

When you're anxious, your brain is stuck in future threats that haven't happened yet. This practice pulls you immediately back to the present moment by engaging all five senses. Your nervous system can't be fully panicked about tomorrow while it's actively processing what's happening right now. The countdown structure gives your spinning mind something concrete to follow.

Use When: Your thoughts are spinning, you feel disconnected from reality, or panic is taking over.

1. Look around and name five things you can *see* out loud. Really look at them.
2. Notice four things you can physically *feel* right now (e.g., your feet on the floor, the chair beneath you, your clothes on your skin, and the air on your face).
3. Listen for three things you can *hear*, even small sounds like the hum of a refrigerator or distant traffic.
4. Identify two things you can *smell* or two smells you like to remember.
5. Name one thing you can *taste* or one taste you enjoy.

MAKE IT YOURS

- Say the items out loud, whisper them, or write them down.
- Go slower and really focus on each sensation if you need more grounding.
- Touch each thing you see to add more sensory input.

Wall Push and Sigh

This practice channels fight-or-flight energy out of your body through safe exertion. The pushing provides grounding and muscular engagement while the sigh signals safety through the vagus nerve. Together, they bring your body back toward balance. When anxiety makes you feel like you're going to jump out of your skin, this gives all that activation somewhere to go.

Use When: You feel buzzy, panicked, or overwhelmed.

1. Stand in front of a wall, feet about hip-width apart.
2. Place your palms flat against the wall at chest or shoulder height.
3. Take a deep breath in through your nose.
4. As you exhale, push into the wall with strong, steady pressure, like you're trying to move it.
5. Let out a long, audible sigh as you push.
6. Pause. Drop your arms. Feel your body.
7. Repeat 3 to 5 times.

MAKE IT YOURS

- No wall nearby? Use a sturdy surface like a countertop, closed door, or even your own thighs.
- Need more release? Add a sound like a growl or *vooooo* on the exhale.
- Pair the exercise with a grounding phrase like "I'm here now" or "I can let go."

Solo Bear Hug

Deep pressure activates your parasympathetic nervous system and signals safety to your brain. When you're anxious and scattered, your body needs the message that you're contained and held. Hugging yourself provides proprioceptive input that helps you feel your boundaries and know where you are in space. You're literally holding yourself through the panic, which your nervous system registers as safety and support.

Use When: You feel scattered, unsafe, or like you're coming apart at the seams.

1. Wrap your arms around yourself in a tight hug, crossing them over your chest.
2. Squeeze yourself firmly, like you're holding yourself together.
3. Hold the squeeze for 10 to 20 seconds while breathing slowly.
4. Gently rock side to side if that feels good, whispering, "I've got you" or "You're safe right now."
5. Stay here as long as you need, and release when you're ready.

MAKE IT YOURS

- Try hugging yourself under a heavy or weighted blanket for even more grounding.
- Add gentle rocking or swaying while you hold yourself.
- Whisper something kind to yourself while you squeeze.

Box Breathing

Box breathing creates equal parts inhale, hold, exhale, and hold, which balances your nervous system and regulates your heart rate. The rhythm and counting give your anxious mind something structured to focus on instead of spiraling. The extended exhales and holds activate your parasympathetic nervous system, telling your body it's safe enough to slow down. This is one of the fastest ways to interrupt a panic response.

Use When: Your heart is racing, your breathing feels shallow or panicked, or you need immediate calm.

1. Sit comfortably.
2. Inhale slowly through your nose for a count of four.
3. Hold your breath gently for a count of four.
4. Exhale slowly through your mouth for a count of four.
5. Hold (while empty) for a count of four.
6. Repeat this cycle 4 to 8 times, or until you feel your system shift.

MAKE IT YOURS

- Adjust the count to what feels comfortable (3 or 5 counts work too).
- Trace an actual box shape with your finger or eyes while you breathe.
- Even two rounds can make a difference if that's all you have time for.

Primal Shake

Animals naturally shake to discharge stress and complete their nervous system's activation cycle after a threat. Humans have this same mechanism, but we've been socialized to suppress it. Getting on all fours and shaking lets your body do what it's been wanting to do all along. This primal movement releases trapped fight-or-flight energy and helps reset your system. It might feel unfamiliar, but it works.

Use When: You feel wired, energy trapped in your body, or like you need to move but don't know how.

1. Get down on your hands and knees on a soft surface.
2. Start shaking your whole body vigorously, like a dog shaking off water after a bath.
3. Let your head, shoulders, torso, and hips all shake loosely and freely.
4. Keep shaking for 20 to 30 seconds, or until you feel the buzzy energy start to settle.
5. Pause, sit back on your heels, and notice how your body feels different.

MAKE IT YOURS

- Try it standing up if getting on the floor feels like too much.
- Add sound such as sighs, growls, or whatever wants to come out while you shake.
- Repeat multiple rounds if once doesn't feel like enough of a discharge.

Back Against the Wall

When you're anxious, your nervous system is scanning for threats from every direction, which keeps you in constant vigilance. Putting a solid surface behind you removes one entire plane of vulnerability. Your brain registers that nothing can come from behind, which allows your nervous system to relax slightly. The physical support of the wall also provides proprioceptive feedback that you're grounded and held.

Use When: You feel exposed, vulnerable, or like threats are coming from all directions.

1. Find a wall and press your back firmly against it.
2. Let your whole spine make contact: your head, shoulders, middle back, and tailbone.
3. Feel the solid surface supporting you from behind.
4. Take 5 to 10 slow breaths here, noticing how your body can rest against something stable.
5. Stay as long as you need, letting the wall hold you up.

MAKE IT YOURS

- Slide down and sit against the wall if standing feels too active.
- Try this in a corner where two walls meet for even more containment.
- Close your eyes if that feels safe or keep them open if you need visual grounding.

Weighted Chest

Deep pressure on your chest activates your parasympathetic nervous system and signals safety to your brain. The weight provides strong proprioceptive feedback that grounds you in your body when anxiety makes you feel scattered or like you're floating away. Breathing against resistance also engages your diaphragm more fully, which stimulates the vagus nerve. This can slow your heart rate and help you feel contained when everything feels too big.

Use When: Your chest feels tight, your breathing is shallow, or you feel ungrounded and floaty.

1. Lie down on your back on a bed, couch, or floor.
2. Place something heavy on your chest, such as a thick book, a weighted blanket, a stack of folded towels, or even a pet if they're willing.
3. Feel the weight pressing down on your sternum and ribs.
4. Breathe slowly and deliberately against the weight, feeling your chest rise and fall.
5. Stay here for 2 to 5 minutes, letting the pressure calm your system.

MAKE IT YOURS:

- Use heavier or lighter weight depending on what feels grounding versus overwhelming.
- Try the weight on your belly instead if your chest feels too vulnerable.
- Place a warm heating pad under the weight for added comfort.

Straw Breathing

The resistance of breathing through a straw automatically extends your exhale, which activates your parasympathetic nervous system. Longer exhales tell your body it's safe to rest. Back-pressure—the gentle pushback you feel as air has to squeeze through a narrow space—also helps regulate your breathing pattern when anxiety has made it shallow and erratic. This technique is particularly powerful because the physical constraint of the straw does the work for you when your brain is too panicked to remember how to breathe slowly.

Use When: You're hyperventilating or breathing too fast.

1. Find a straw (or pretend you have one by pursing your lips tightly).
2. Inhale normally through your nose.
3. Exhale slowly and completely through the straw (or pursed lips), letting it take as long as possible.
4. The narrow opening forces you to extend your exhale, and the resistance of pushing air through a small space helps stabilize erratic breathing.
5. Repeat for 5 to 10 breaths, or until you feel your system start to settle.

MAKE IT YOURS

- Try different straw widths; a narrower straw creates more resistance and slower exhales.
- Combine with counting your exhales to give your mind something to focus on.
- Even three breaths taken this way can shift your state if that's all you can manage.

Throw It Away

Your body wants to push away or get rid of what's threatening you, but anxiety often feels like something you can't escape. This throwing gesture gives your nervous system a physical action to complete that impulse. The overhead to downward motion engages your core and creates a full-body discharge. Making the invisible visible through movement helps your brain process that you're actively doing something about the overwhelm.

Use When: You feel burdened, carrying too much, or need to release something you can't control.

1. Stand with your feet hip-width apart.
2. Imagine gathering up all the anxiety, worry, or overwhelm in your hands.
3. Raise your arms overhead like you're holding a heavy ball, then hurl it down and away from you, letting your hands fly open at the release.
4. Let your whole body follow the motion.
5. Repeat 5 to 10 times or until your arms feel tired and the charge decreases.

MAKE IT YOURS

- Add sound with each throw—grunt, yell, or exhale forcefully.
- Name what you're throwing away, and state it out loud if that helps (e.g., "My worry!" or "That meeting!" or "All of it!").
- Do this exercise sitting if standing feels like too much.

Left Nostril Breathing

Your left nostril is directly connected to the right hemisphere of your brain and your parasympathetic nervous system, while your right nostril is directly connected to the left hemisphere and your sympathetic nervous system. When you are anxious, the right nostril is often dominant. Breathing through only your left nostril activates the calming, rest-and-digest response in your body. This ancient yogic technique is grounded in neuroscience—it literally shifts your nervous system from sympathetic activation to parasympathetic settling in one fell swoop.

Use When: You're wired, can't slow down, or need to activate your calming system quickly.

1. Sit comfortably and use your right thumb to gently close your right nostril.
2. Breathe in slowly and gently through your left nostril only.
3. Close your left nostril with your right ring finger and release your right nostril.
4. Exhale slowly through your right nostril.
5. Repeat this pattern for 2 to 3 minutes: inhale left, and exhale right.

MAKE IT YOURS

- If the hand position feels awkward, press any finger against your left nostril to close it.
- Do fewer rounds if you feel lightheaded (1 to 2 minutes can be enough).
- If you have difficulty breathing through your nose, place your hand over the left side of your chest and breathe slowly while focusing your attention there. You'll still activate the calming response through intention and attention.

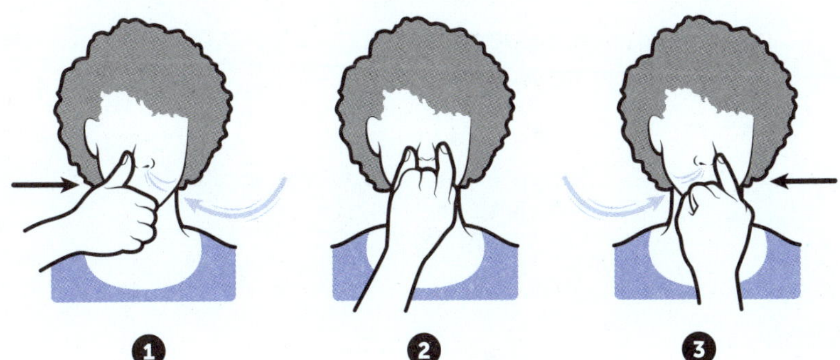

Scent Cue Ritual

Scent bypasses your thinking brain and connects directly to your limbic system, which processes emotion and memory. When you pair a specific scent with moments of regulation, you create an anchor your nervous system recognizes. Over time, just smelling it can begin to shift your state. The ritual aspect matters too; having a consistent response to anxiety helps your brain feel less out of control. You're giving yourself something concrete to rely on when everything feels chaotic.

Use When: You're spiraling, need an immediate anchor, or want to interrupt the panic loop.

1. Choose a specific scent you associate with calm or safety—perhaps lavender, peppermint, coffee, citrus, or a certain perfume.
2. Keep it in a convenient spot such as your pocket, purse, desk drawer, or car.
3. When anxiety hits, bring the scent to your nose and take three slow, deliberate breaths.
4. As you inhale, remind yourself, "I've been here before. I know how to get through this."
5. Let the scent become your signal that you're taking care of yourself.

MAKE IT YOURS

- Use essential oil, scented lotion, tea, fresh herbs, or anything with a distinct smell.
- Keep multiple sources of your chosen scent in different locations.
- Practice using it when you're calm so the association strengthens.

Sprint and Ground

When you're anxious, your body is flooded with adrenaline and cortisol, preparing you to flee. Running gives that energy the outlet it's screaming for. The sudden stop after intense movement creates a powerful contrast that helps your nervous system register the shift from activation to stillness. Standing still afterward with awareness helps ground all that discharge and signals to your body that the threat has passed. You're completing the flight response your system was stuck in.

Use When: You have explosive anxiety energy and need to discharge it before you can settle.

1. Stand with enough space to move your legs.
2. Start running in place: Lift your knees, pump your arms, and go fast.
3. Run hard for 30 to 60 seconds, letting the energy move through you.
4. Stop suddenly and plant your feet firmly on the ground.
5. Stand completely still and notice everything: your heartbeat, your breathing, the ground beneath you, and how your body feels different.
6. Notice the difference in your body before and after; that's your nervous system resetting.

MAKE IT YOURS:

- Try jumping jacks or high knees instead if running in place feels awkward.
- Do this outside if you have space and privacy.
- Add sound, such as heavy exhales or grunting, while you run for more release.

Grounded Drop

Impact grounds you literally and neurologically. When you're anxious and dissociated, your proprioceptive system (knowing where you are in space) gets disrupted. Jumping and landing sends strong signals through your joints and bones that tell your brain exactly where your body is. The vestibular activation from going up and down also helps organize your nervous system. Each heavy landing is like hitting a reset button that says, "I'm here, I'm solid, I'm on the ground."

Use When: You feel ungrounded, floaty, or disconnected from your body.

1. Stand with your feet hip-width apart.
2. Jump up, not high, just a few inches off the ground.
3. Land with your whole foot flat and heavy, knees slightly bent.
4. Feel the impact through your legs and feet.
5. Repeat 10 to 15 times, focusing on the sensation of landing solidly each time.

MAKE IT YOURS

- Try stomping hard instead if jumping isn't accessible.
- Land and pause between jumps to really feel the grounding.
- Do this barefoot on a natural surface, if possible, for even more connection.

Butterfly Hug

The butterfly hug uses bilateral stimulation, the same mechanism used in EMDR therapy, a treatment that uses sensory input to process traumatic memories and reduce distress. Alternating taps on each side of your body helps integrate your left and right brain hemispheres, which can feel fragmented during anxiety. The self-hold provides comfort while the rhythmic tapping organizes your nervous system. You're literally holding and soothing yourself through the overwhelm, which signals safety to your brain.

Use When: You're overwhelmed, need self-soothing, or feel like you're falling apart.

1. Cross your arms over your chest, placing your right hand on your left shoulder and your left hand on your right shoulder.
2. Begin tapping alternately: right hand, left hand, right hand, left hand.
3. Keep a slow, gentle rhythm like a heartbeat.
4. Continue for 1 to 2 minutes, breathing slowly as you tap.
5. Notice if anything shifts: your breathing, your thoughts, or the intensity of your feelings.

MAKE IT YOURS

- Try tapping on your upper arms instead of your shoulders if that's more comfortable.
- Combine with a gentle phrase like "I'm here" or "I'm safe" with each tap.
- Do this lying down if sitting feels too active.

Gargling

Gargling activates the muscles in the back of your throat that are directly connected to the vagus nerve. The vigorous vibration stimulates the vagus nerve, which sends calming signals to your brain and helps shift you out of sympathetic activation. It might feel clunky or unglamorous, but it's one of the fastest ways to manually activate your parasympathetic nervous system. The sensory intensity also interrupts anxious thought loops because your brain can't focus on worrying while you're gargling loudly.

Use When: You feel anxious, stuck in your throat, or need a quick vagal nerve reset.

1. Get a glass of water, stand in front of a sink, and take a sip without swallowing.
2. Tilt your head back slightly and gargle as vigorously as you can.
3. Really make it loud and active; let your throat shake and vibrate.
4. Spit or swallow, then repeat.
5. Do 3 to 5 rounds of gargling, feeling the sensation in your throat with each one.
6. Notice if you feel calmer, yawn, or take a deeper breath afterward; those are signs it's working.

MAKE IT YOURS

- Gargle harder and louder for more vagal stimulation.
- Try this in the shower or bathroom, where you can be as loud as you want.
- Use cold water for added nervous system activation.

CHAPTER 8

When You Need to Sleep or Settle

You're tired. You want to sleep. Your body should be ready. But instead, you're lying there staring at the ceiling while your brain runs through tomorrow's to-do list, that conversation from three days ago, and whether you remembered to lock the front door.

If this is your experience right now, you're not bad at sleeping—your nervous system is stuck in activation mode even though the actual stressors are done for the day. You're tired but wired, physically exhausted but mentally buzzing, restless in a way that makes no sense given how much you need rest. Your body seems to have forgotten how to relax.

Here's what's happening: Your brain hasn't gotten the message that it's safe to rest. The activation has come down from where it was earlier, but it's not low enough yet for your body to fully let go. You're in that frustrating in-between space—too tired to do anything but too wired to sleep.

This is incredibly common, and it's not a willpower problem. Your nervous system doesn't operate on your schedule. It doesn't know that you have to be up at 6 a.m. or that you've already done everything you can about tomorrow's meeting. It's still scanning, still processing, still running its background programs because no one told it the day is actually over.

The practices in this chapter are designed to send that signal. They help your body complete the transition from doing to resting, from activation to settling. Think of them as closing rituals for your nervous system—clear evidence that threats have passed, the day is done, and it's finally safe to let your guard down.

It's time to help your body remember it's safe to rest.

Physiological Sigh

The physiological sigh is one of the fastest ways to calm your nervous system. The double inhale fully expands the air sacs in your lungs and offloads carbon dioxide while the long exhale activates your vagus nerve. This breathing pattern naturally occurs when you're crying or relieved, and doing it intentionally signals to your brain that the stressor has passed and it's time to settle. Stanford research shows this is more effective than meditation for immediate stress reduction.

Use When: You feel tense, anxious, or need to signal to your body that it's safe to wind down.

1. Sit or lie comfortably.
2. Take a deep inhale through your nose, filling your lungs about 80 percent.
3. Without exhaling, take a quick second inhale through your nose to top off your lungs completely.
4. Exhale slowly and fully through your mouth with a long sigh.
5. Repeat 2 to 3 times, feeling your body soften with each cycle.

MAKE IT YOURS

- Make the exhale even longer if you need more calming.
- Try this in bed as part of your wind-down routine.
- Pair the sigh with placing a hand on your heart for added soothing.

Legs up the Wall

Inverting your legs reverses blood flow and activates the pressure sensors in your neck, which signal your brain to activate the parasympathetic nervous system. This gentle inversion helps drain tension from your legs, reduces cortisol, and shifts your body into rest mode. The supported nature of this pose makes it deeply restorative without requiring any effort. Your body literally gets the message that it's time to restore and recover.

Use When: You feel restless, wired, or physically exhausted but can't settle.

Caution: Skip this one if you have glaucoma, uncontrolled high blood pressure, or are in late pregnancy—try lying flat with a pillow under your knees instead.

1. Lie on your back near a wall and scoot your hips as close to the wall as comfortable.
2. Extend your legs up the wall, letting them rest there fully supported.
3. Place your arms out to the sides, palms up, or rest your hands on your belly.
4. Close your eyes and breathe naturally for 5 to 15 minutes.
5. To come out, bend your knees and roll gently to one side before sitting up.

MAKE IT YOURS

- Move your hips farther from the wall if the stretch feels too intense.
- Try this with a weighted eye pillow for deeper relaxation.
- Make this part of your bedtime routine every night for cumulative benefits.

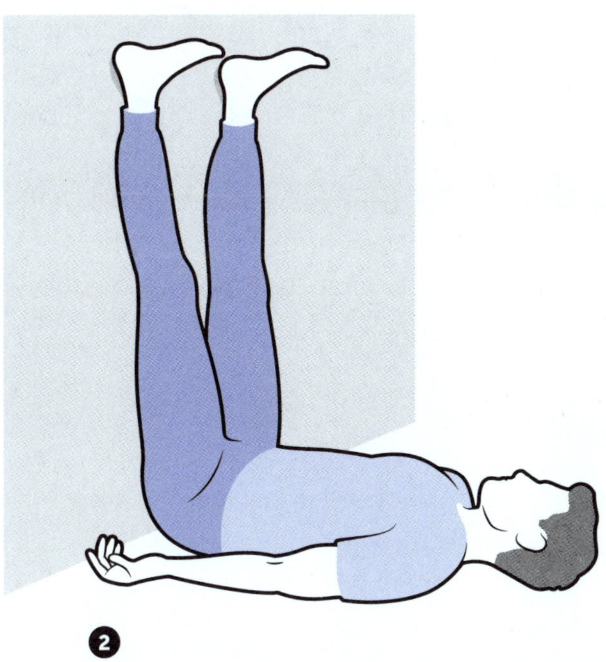

2

Progressive Muscle Relaxation

Developed in the 1920s and extensively researched since, progressive muscle relaxation (PMR) reduces cortisol, lowers blood pressure, and signals your nervous system to shift into rest mode. It teaches your body the difference between tension and release by exaggerating both states. When you squeeze muscles then let go, they relax more deeply than they would on their own. This practice also brings awareness to where you're holding tension unconsciously. It's particularly effective for sleep because it systematically releases the physical holding patterns that keep you awake.

Use When: You're holding physical tension, can't stop clenching, or your body won't let go.

1. Lie down or sit comfortably in a quiet space.
2. Starting with your feet, tense all the muscles as tightly as you can for 5 seconds.
3. Release completely and notice the difference between tension and relaxation.
4. Move up through your body: calves, thighs, glutes, stomach, chest, hands, arms, shoulders, neck, and face.
5. Tense each area for 5 seconds, then release fully before moving to the next.

MAKE IT YOURS

- Spend more time on areas that hold the most tension such as the jaw, shoulders, and forehead.
- Do just your upper body or lower body if a full scan feels too long.
- Follow with a few minutes of lying still to let the relaxation deepen.

Bumblebee Breath

This breath creates internal vibration that directly stimulates the vagus nerve and activates the parasympathetic nervous system. Closing your ears amplifies the sound inside your head, which drowns out external noise and internal mental chatter. The low-frequency humming has been shown to reduce blood pressure, slow heart rate, and decrease anxiety. In yogic tradition, this is called Bhramari breath, named after the black Indian bee; it is considered one of the most effective practices for calming an agitated mind before sleep.

Use When: Your mind won't stop racing, you feel agitated, or need deep internal calming.

1. Sit comfortably or lie down with your eyes closed, if that feels safe.
2. Place your index fingers gently over your ear openings (or use your thumbs).
3. Take a deep breath in through your nose.
4. As you exhale, make a low, steady humming sound like a bee: *Mmmmmmm.*
5. Feel the vibration in your head and chest. Repeat 5 to 10 times.

MAKE IT YOURS

- Try different pitches to find what creates the most vibration and calm.
- Skip covering your ears if that feels claustrophobic.
- Combine with gentle rocking for added soothing.

Acupressure Points

These acupressure points have been used for centuries in traditional Chinese medicine (TCM) to promote sleep and calm the nervous system. Modern research confirms that stimulating these points releases endorphins, reduces cortisol, and activates parasympathetic pathways. The gentle pressure combined with focused attention helps redirect your mind away from racing thoughts while your body receives direct signals to relax. The repetitive nature of moving through the points also creates a calming ritual that prepares your brain for sleep.

Use When: You can't turn off your mind, feel physically tense, or need help initiating sleep.

1. Lie down or sit comfortably in a dimly lit space.
2. Use your fingertips to apply gentle, circular pressure to these points for 30 to 60 seconds each:
    - between your eyebrows (third eye point)
    - behind your earlobes in the small hollow
    - base of your skull where it meets your neck
    - center of your wrists on the palm side
3. Breathe slowly as you press each point.
4. Move through all the points, then repeat if needed.

MAKE IT YOURS

- Add a drop of lavender oil to your fingertips before starting.
- Make this a consistent bedtime ritual so your body learns to associate it with sleep.
- Focus on just one or two points if doing all of them feels overwhelming.

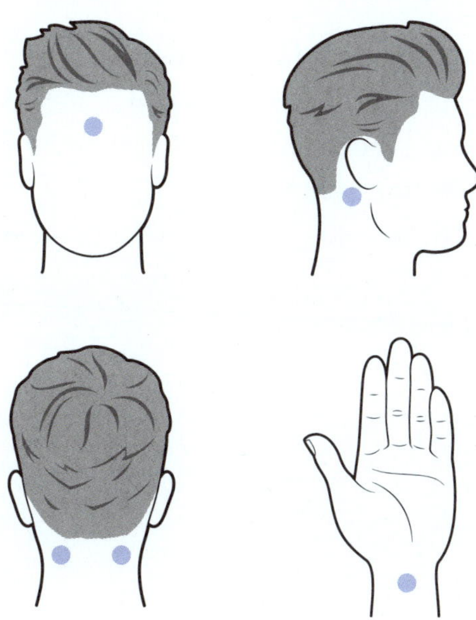

Supine Spinal Twist

Gentle spinal twists release tension held in your back and torso while stimulating your parasympathetic nervous system. The rotation wrings out physical and energetic holding patterns, and the opposing head turn creates a fuller release through your spine. This pose also gently compresses and releases your organs, which can aid digestion and help your body shift into rest mode. The supported, passive nature of this twist makes it ideal for bedtime because it requires no effort while still providing significant release.

Use When: Your back feels tight, you're holding tension in your torso, or need a gentle release.

1. Lie on your back with your knees bent and feet flat.
2. Extend your arms out to the sides in a T shape, palms up.
3. Let both knees fall slowly to the right side, keeping your shoulders on the ground.
4. Turn your head to the left (opposite direction of your knees).
5. Hold for 1 to 3 minutes, breathing deeply, then switch sides.

MAKE IT YOURS

- Place a pillow between your knees for more support and comfort.
- Hold for longer on whichever side feels tighter.
- Skip the head turn if it feels uncomfortable for your neck.

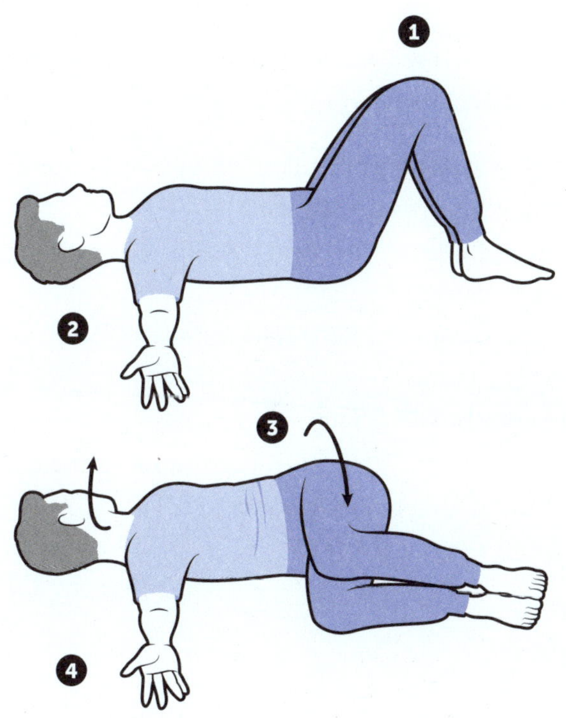

4-7-8 Breathing Pattern

Developed by Dr. Andrew Weil, the 4-7-8 breath is often called a "natural tranquilizer for the nervous system." The extended hold and long exhale dramatically increases oxygen in your bloodstream and activates your parasympathetic nervous system. The specific ratio forces you to slow your breathing below your normal rate, which signals to your brain that you're safe and it's time to rest. Many people report falling asleep before completing four cycles. With practice, this becomes more effective as your body learns to associate the pattern with sleep.

Use When: You can't fall asleep, feel anxious in bed, or need a fast-acting sedative technique.

1. Lie in bed or sit comfortably with your tongue resting behind your upper front teeth.
2. Exhale completely through your mouth with a *whoosh* sound.
3. Close your mouth and inhale quietly through your nose for a count of four.
4. Hold your breath for a count of seven.
5. Exhale completely through your mouth for a count of eight, making a *whoosh* sound.
6. Repeat this cycle 3 to 4 times.

MAKE IT YOURS

- Adjust the counts slightly if the ratio feels uncomfortable (3-5-6 works too).
- Skip the *whoosh* sound if you share a bedroom and it feels disruptive.
- Use this in the middle of the night if you wake up and can't fall back asleep.

Deep Belly Breathing

Diaphragmatic breathing, also called belly breathing, is the foundation of all calming breath work. When you're stressed, you tend to breathe shallowly from your chest, which keeps your nervous system activated. Breathing from your diaphragm engages the vagus nerve, slows your heart rate, and signals safety to your brain. Relearning this pattern restores your body's natural rest response and is particularly effective for sleep because it creates the slow, deep breathing pattern your body associates with deep rest.

Use When: Your breathing feels shallow, you're chest-breathing from stress, or need foundational calming.

1. Lie on your back with one hand on your chest and one on your belly.
2. Breathe in slowly through your nose, directing the breath down so your belly rises while your chest stays relatively still.
3. Feel your hand on your belly lift as your diaphragm expands downward.
4. Exhale slowly through your mouth, feeling your belly fall.
5. Continue for 5 to 10 minutes, keeping your breath slow and deep.

MAKE IT YOURS

- Place a light book on your belly to give yourself visual feedback as it rises and falls.
- Make your exhales longer than your inhales for a more calming effect.
- If you lose focus, just return to watching your belly rise and fall.

Constructive Rest

Constructive rest position aligns your skeleton in a way that requires zero muscular effort to maintain. Your body can completely let go because your bones are stacked and supported. This positioning releases tension in your hip flexors, psoas muscles, lower back, and pelvic floor—areas that hold tremendous stress. Developed by dancer Lulu Sweigard in the 1930s and used in somatic practices since, this position allows your nervous system to reset without you having to do anything. The effortlessness is the point; your body learns it's safe to stop working and just be.

Use When: Your body is exhausted but won't settle, or you need passive restoration.

1. Lie on your back on a firm surface such as the floor or bed.
2. Bend your knees and place your feet flat, hip-width apart, and a comfortable distance from your hips.
3. Let your knees lean into each other for support, creating a stable triangle with your legs.
4. Place your arms by your sides or rest your hands on your belly.
5. Close your eyes and rest here for 5 to 10 minutes, allowing gravity to do all the work.

MAKE IT YOURS

- Place a pillow or folded blanket under your head if that's more comfortable.
- Adjust the distance of your feet from your hips until you feel fully supported.
- If your knees don't naturally lean together, place a block or pillow between them.

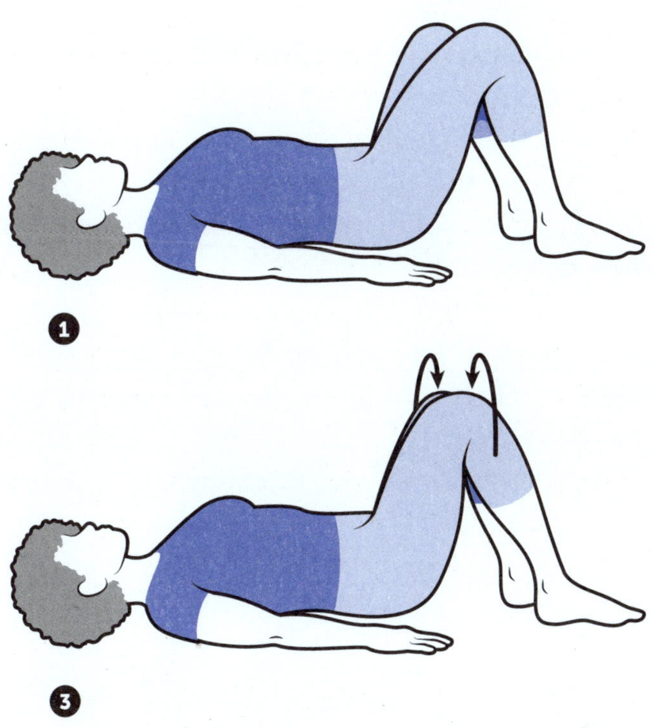

Alternate Nostril Breathing

Alternate nostril breathing balances the left and right hemispheres of your brain and regulates both branches of your autonomic nervous system. Your left nostril activates your parasympathetic (calming) system while your right activates your sympathetic (alerting) system. By alternating, you create equilibrium. Research shows this practice reduces heart rate, lowers blood pressure, and decreases anxiety. In yogic tradition, it's considered one of the most powerful techniques for calming the mind before meditation or sleep because it balances your nervous system.

Use When: You feel imbalanced, your mind won't settle, or you need deep nervous system regulation.

1. Sit comfortably or lie down with your spine relatively straight.
2. Use your right thumb to gently close your right nostril.
3. Inhale slowly through your left nostril.
4. Close your left nostril with your right ring finger, release your right nostril.
5. Exhale slowly through your right nostril.
6. Inhale through your right nostril.
7. Close your right nostril, release your left nostril, exhale through your left.
8. This completes one round. Continue for 5 to 10 rounds.

MAKE IT YOURS

- If the hand position feels awkward, use one finger to close each nostril.
- Make the exhales slightly longer than the inhales for a more calming effect.
- If breathing through your nose is difficult, try alternating the hand resting on your chest with each breath—left hand for inhale, right hand for exhale—to create a similar balancing effect through touch instead.

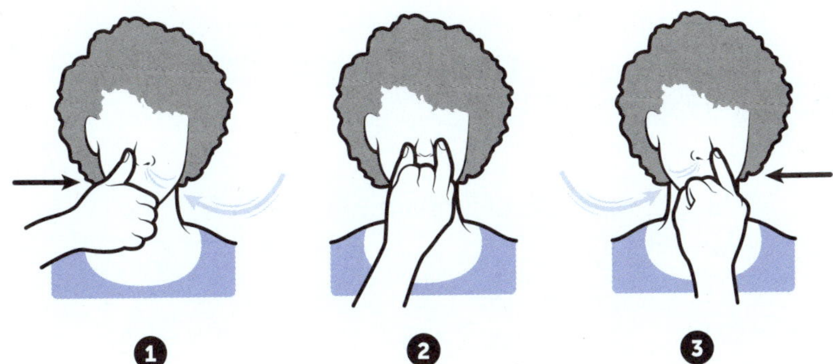

Knees-to-Chest Compression

Bringing your knees to your chest releases tension in your lower back, hips, hip flexors, and psoas muscles, areas that hold stress from sitting, standing, and emotional tension. The gentle compression also stimulates your vagus nerve through pressure on your abdomen, which activates your parasympathetic nervous system. This pose improves circulation to your digestive organs and can help relieve gas and bloating that might keep you awake. The fetal position is inherently calming and signals safety to your body, making it an ideal pre-sleep posture.

Use When: Your lower back is tense, you feel compressed from the day, or need gentle release.

1. Lie on your back on a comfortable surface with your legs bent and feet flat on the floor.
2. Draw both knees toward your chest, wrapping your arms around your shins.
3. Hold your knees gently but firmly, feeling compression in your lower back and hips.
4. Rock gently from side to side if that feels good, massaging your lower back.
5. Hold for 1 to 3 minutes, breathing deeply into the compression.

MAKE IT YOURS

- Hold one knee at a time if bringing both up feels too intense for your back.
- Rock more vigorously if your back needs deeper massage.
- Follow with legs extended flat to feel the contrast and release.

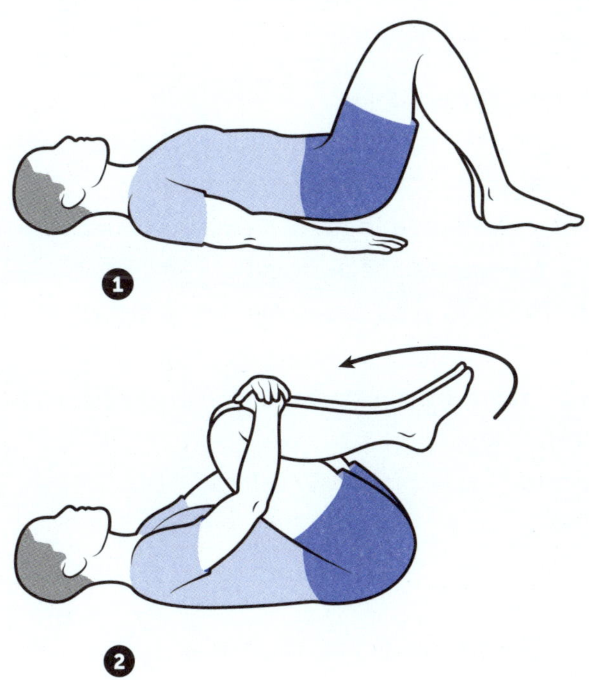

Autogenic Training

Autogenic training, developed in the 1930s by psychiatrist Johannes Schultz, uses self-suggestion to create physiological changes in your body. When you repeatedly suggest heaviness and warmth, your muscles actually relax and blood flow increases. This isn't imagination; studies show autogenic training reduces cortisol, lowers heart rate, and improves sleep quality. The systematic progression through your body gives your mind a structured task while your body responds to the suggestions. It's like guided self-hypnosis that teaches your nervous system to shift into deep rest on command.

Use When: Your body won't relax despite being exhausted, or you need deep systematic calming.

1. Lie down comfortably.
2. Focus on your right arm and silently repeat, "My right arm is heavy and warm," for 30 to 60 seconds.
3. Move through your body systematically: left arm, right leg, left leg, repeating the phrases.
4. Then focus on your heartbeat: "My heartbeat is calm and regular."
5. Finally, focus on your breathing: "My breathing is slow and effortless."
6. End with "I am completely calm."

MAKE IT YOURS

- Spend more time on phrases that resonate with your body.
- Do just the upper body if the full sequence feels too long.
- Record yourself saying the phrases and play it back as you fall asleep.

Parasympathetic Yawn

Yawning is one of your body's natural mechanisms for regulating your nervous system and brain temperature. When you yawn, you stimulate the vagus nerve, increase oxygen intake, and release tension in your jaw and face, areas that hold tremendous stress. Yawning is contagious even with yourself; intentionally triggering one often leads to real ones. Research shows yawning before bed increases parasympathetic activity and prepares your brain for sleep. It's also a sign your body is already starting to wind down, so encouraging more yawning accelerates that process.

Use When: You feel tense in your face and jaw, or need a quick nervous system reset.

1. Sit or lie comfortably and open your mouth wide.
2. Fake a yawn by stretching your jaw open and inhaling deeply.
3. Let the fake yawn trigger a real one if possible; your body often follows.
4. Don't hold back; let the yawn be big, loud, and satisfying.
5. Repeat 3 to 5 times, or until real yawns start happening naturally.

MAKE IT YOURS

- Really exaggerate the yawn to make it more likely to trigger real ones.
- Stretch your arms overhead while yawning for a full-body release.
- Massage your jaw before or after if it feels particularly tight.

Supported Child's Pose

Supported child's pose creates gentle compression on your abdomen, which stimulates the vagus nerve and activates your parasympathetic nervous system. The forward fold naturally slows your heart rate and deepens your breathing. Resting your forehead on a surface activates pressure points that calm your nervous system. The surrender position, bowing down and releasing effort, sends powerful signals to your brain that it's safe to let go. With full support under your body, you can completely release muscular tension and allow gravity to do all the work.

Use When: You feel overwhelmed, need to surrender, or want full-body grounding and release.

1. Kneel on your bed or a soft surface with your knees wide apart.
2. Place a pillow, bolster, or folded blankets under your torso for full support.
3. Bring your big toes to touch behind you.
4. Fold forward, extending your arms out in front or resting them by your sides.
5. Rest your forehead on the surface and breathe here for 3 to 10 minutes, or as long as you need to experience deep rest.

MAKE IT YOURS

- Keep your knees closer together if them being wide feels uncomfortable for your hips.
- Place a rolled towel behind your knees if you have knee sensitivity.
- Turn your head to one side if forehead down feels claustrophobic.

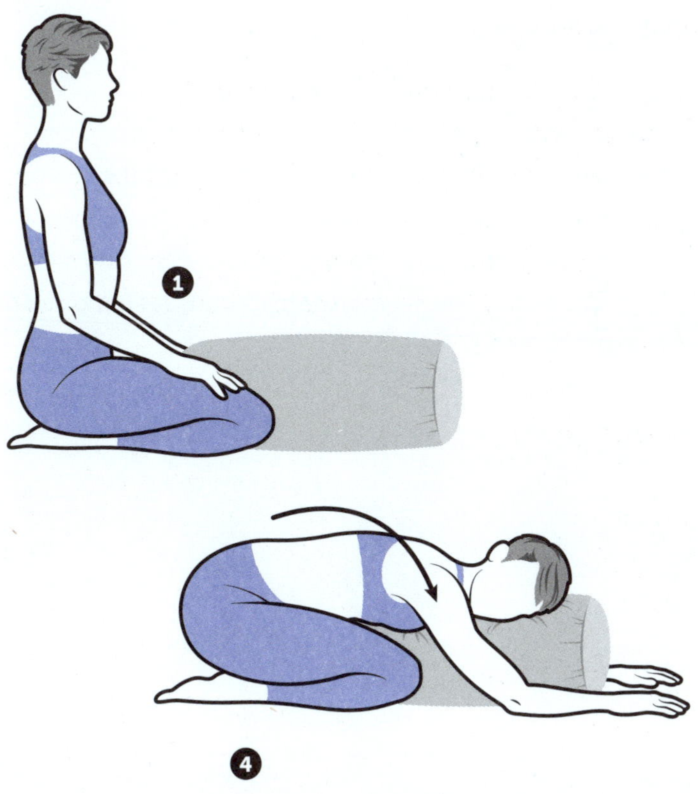

Rotation Release

This gentle rotation creates subtle movement through your entire body without requiring effort or activation. The internal rotation of your legs from the hip joint releases tension in your hip flexors and lower back. Turning your head stimulates your vestibular system (balance and spatial awareness) in a calming way. The alternating pattern creates a soothing rhythm while the minimal movement satisfies your body's need to shift and settle without waking you up further. This practice is particularly helpful when you're restless but too tired for anything more active.

Use When: You feel restless, can't get comfortable, or need gentle full-body movement.

1. Lie on your back with your legs extended.
2. Starting with your feet in a relaxed, neutral position, gently rotate both legs inward from your hips so your big toes move toward each other.
3. At the same time, slowly turn your head to one side.
4. Hold for 10 to 20 seconds, then let your feet and head return to center.
5. Repeat the inward rotation while turning your head to the other side.

MAKE IT YOURS

- Move even slower if the rhythm feels too fast.
- Try just the leg rotations or just the head turns if doing both feels complicated.
- Add a gentle rock or sway while you rotate if that feels good.

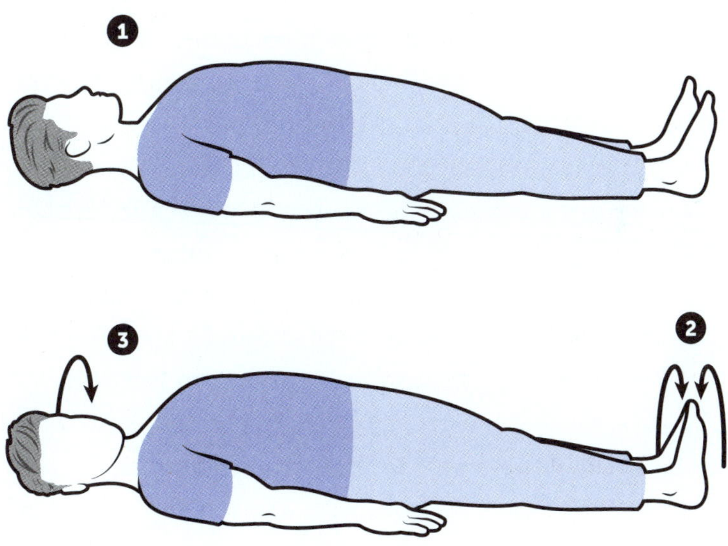

CHAPTER 9

When You Need Connection

You feel alone. Not necessarily lonely, but disconnected—from yourself, from others, from the world around you. Maybe you've been isolating, or maybe you're surrounded by people but still feel like you're watching life happen from behind glass. Either way, something that used to feel natural now feels impossibly far away.

If this is where you are, you might be feeling isolated, emotionally numb, or like connection is possible for other people but not for you right now. You might crave contact but have no idea how to reach for it. You might feel unlovable or like everyone else has something you don't. The thought of opening up to someone might sound exhausting, terrifying, or just completely out of reach.

Here's what's happening: Your nervous system has moved away from ventral vagal engagement—the state where connection feels safe and possible. When you're disconnected like this, it's usually because your system doesn't feel safe enough for the vulnerability that connection requires. You might be protecting yourself by staying separate, or you might genuinely not know how to reach out anymore. Either way, your social engagement system has gone offline, and that's why connection feels so hard right now. It's not a character flaw. And it's not permanent. It's a nervous system state.

The practices in this chapter are designed to help your system remember that connection is available—that it's safe to reach out and that you belong in relationship with others and the world around you. Some involve other people or living beings, but many can be done alone while still activating your capacity for connection. You don't have to force yourself into socializing before you're ready.

You're not as alone as you feel. Let's help you find your way back.

Intentional Smile

The facial feedback hypothesis shows that your facial expressions don't just reflect your emotions, they actually create them. When you smile, even artificially, you activate the same neural pathways as a genuine smile, which releases endorphins and serotonin. Smiling also signals to your nervous system that you're safe enough to be open and receptive, which activates your ventral vagal (social engagement) system. This practice can feel uncomfortable if you're deeply disconnected, but that discomfort is information about how far you've moved from connection.

Use When: You feel disconnected, flat, or like you've forgotten how to feel warmth.

1. Sit or stand in front of a mirror, or just notice your face.
2. Gently turn the corners of your mouth up into a soft smile.
3. Hold the smile for 30 to 60 seconds, even if it feels forced or fake.
4. Notice any shifts in how you feel: perhaps warmth, lightness, or even resistance.
5. Let the smile soften naturally, then try again if you want.

MAKE IT YOURS

- Start with just 10 seconds if any more feels too long or fake.
- Try smiling with your eyes (crinkling the corners) for a more genuine feeling.
- Notice if smiling at others (even strangers) shifts your sense of belonging.

Auditory Co-Regulation

Your nervous system co-regulates through vocal tone and prosody—the rhythm and melody of speech. When you hear a calm, safe voice, your own nervous system begins to match that state. This is why talking to certain people makes you feel instantly better. The vagus nerve has direct connections to your ears and vocal cords, so you don't even have to share what's wrong—simply listening to safe voices activates your social engagement system and can shift your state.

Use When: You feel isolated, crave human connection, or need to hear a safe voice.

1. Think of someone who feels safe and grounding to you.
2. Call or video chat them with a simple request: "Can I just listen to you talk for a few minutes?"
3. Ask them to tell you about their day, something they're interested in, or anything that comes to mind.
4. Focus on the sound and rhythm of their voice, not necessarily the content.
5. Let their regulated nervous system help regulate yours through their tone and presence.
6. Notice how your breathing and heart rate shift as you listen.

MAKE IT YOURS

- Let them know you don't need advice or problem-solving, just their voice.
- Try this with different safe people to notice whose voice regulates you most.
- Record a safe person talking so you can listen when they're not available.

Acupressure Hug

This self-hold activates acupressure points while creating the sensation of being embraced. The pressure under your left arm stimulates lymphatic flow and calming points, while the crossed-arm position mimics being held by another person. Your nervous system responds to the compression and warmth as it would to an actual hug, releasing oxytocin and activating your parasympathetic system. The elbows falling inward creates containment and safety. When human touch isn't available or doesn't feel safe, this practice provides similar regulatory benefits through your own body.

Use When: You crave being held, feel alone, or need deep self-soothing.

1. Cross your arms in front of your body.
2. Place your right hand under your left armpit, wrapping your left arm around toward your right shoulder.
3. Let your elbows fall toward your center, creating gentle compression.
4. Hold this position for 1 to 3 minutes, breathing slowly and deeply.
5. Notice the pressure, warmth, and sense of being held.

MAKE IT YOURS

- Reverse the arm that is on top to see if one side feels more comforting.
- Rock gently while holding yourself for added soothing.
- Add a phrase like "I'm here" or "You're safe" while you hold.

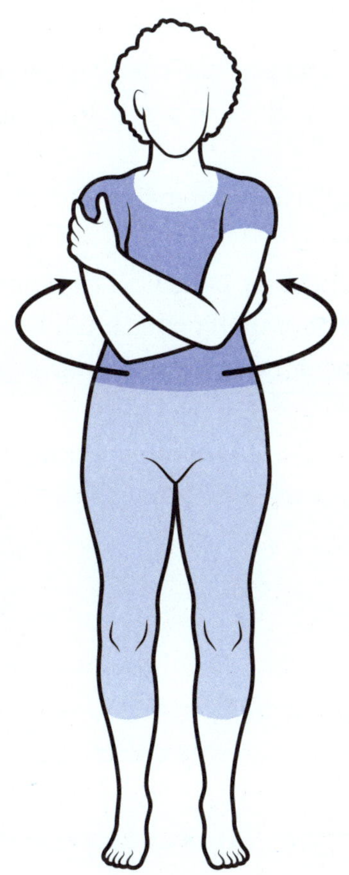

Nature Watching

Observing animal behavior activates your social engagement system even though you're not directly interacting; your brain recognizes life and movement. Studies show that watching wildlife reduces stress, increases feelings of connection, and can lift depression. You're witnessing a world that continues regardless of your pain, which can be both humbling and deeply comforting.

Use When: You feel disconnected from life, isolated, or need to witness something beyond yourself.

1. Find a spot where you can observe wildlife: through a window, in a park, or in any outdoor space you can access.
2. Sit quietly and just watch their movements without trying to do anything.
3. Notice their rhythms, behaviors, and how they interact with each other or their environment.
4. Let yourself be curious about their lives happening in the same moment as yours.
5. Stay for at least 5 to 10 minutes, letting their aliveness register in your system.

MAKE IT YOURS

- Set up a bird feeder outside your window for consistent connection opportunities.
- Watch wildlife videos or live animal cams if you can't access nature directly.
- Notice which animals or behaviors are most soothing to watch.

Prosocial Messaging

Prosocial behavior (doing something kind for others) activates reward centers in your brain and releases oxytocin, even when it's as simple as sending a text. The act of reaching out, regardless of response, moves you from isolation toward connection. It practices vulnerability and reminds you that you exist in relationship to others. Research shows that initiating social contact, even digitally, reduces loneliness and activates your social engagement system. You're also potentially creating connection for the other person, which can create a positive feedback loop when they respond warmly.

Use When: You want connection but feel too overwhelmed for real-time interaction.

1. Think of someone you care about but haven't connected with recently.
2. Send them a simple, genuine message like "Just thinking of you," "Hope you're having a good day," or "I appreciate you because . . ."
3. Don't wait for the perfect words. Keep it short and authentic.
4. Send it without expectation of immediate response.
5. Notice how reaching out, even in this small way, shifts something in you.

MAKE IT YOURS

- Share something specific you appreciate about them rather than generic pleasantries.
- Try voice messages if typing feels too formal or distant.
- Notice which responses make you feel most connected and seek more of those relationships.

Relational Mirroring

Mirroring activates mirror neurons in your brain, which are specifically designed to help you understand and connect with others. When you move in sync with someone, your nervous systems begin to co-regulate and attune to each other. This practice creates felt connection without requiring words or emotional processing. Synchronized movement releases oxytocin and creates a sense of being seen and understood. Mirroring is how infants first learn connection with caregivers, and practicing it as an adult can access that primal sense of relational safety and attunement.

Use When: You're with someone safe and want to deepen connection through presence.

1. Sit or stand facing someone you trust.
2. One person begins making slow, simple movements such as raising arms, swaying, or gentle gestures.
3. The other person mirrors those movements as closely as possible.
4. Switch roles after 2 to 3 minutes so the other person leads.
5. Move slowly and stay present with each other throughout.

MAKE IT YOURS

- Try this with music playing in the background for added rhythm.
- Notice how it feels to lead versus following; both require a different type of vulnerability.
- Try this in a group setting.

Tree Connection

Trees are living systems with measurable electromagnetic fields that your nervous system can attune to. Research shows that physical contact with trees reduces cortisol, lowers blood pressure, and activates parasympathetic responses. The solid, rooted presence of a tree provides a felt sense of stability when everything else feels chaotic. You're co-regulating with a living being that isn't asking anything of you, which can feel safer than human connection when you're especially overwhelmed.

Use When: You feel untethered, alone, or disconnected from something larger than yourself.

1. Find a tree in your yard, at a park, or along a street.
2. Stand or sit with your back against the trunk, or place your hands on the bark.
3. Close your eyes, if that feels safe, and notice the solidity and presence of the tree.
4. Feel its aliveness. Notice the rough texture, the temperature, and the sense of something living and breathing.
5. Stay for 3 to 5 minutes, letting yourself be supported or held by something steadier and perhaps much older than you.

MAKE IT YOURS

- Return to the same tree regularly to deepen your relationship with it.
- Hug the tree if that feels natural, or simply lean against it.
- Bring your attention to the tree's roots beneath you, grounding into earth.

Mirror Gaze

Mirror gazing is a powerful practice for reconnecting with yourself when you've become a stranger to your own experience. Sustained eye contact, even with yourself, activates your social engagement system and can create feelings of connection and compassion. Research on mirror meditation shows it increases self-compassion, reduces self-criticism, and helps people feel more present in their own lives.

Use When: You feel disconnected from yourself, invisible, or like you've disappeared.

1. Sit comfortably in front of a mirror where you can see your face clearly.
2. Look into your own eyes for 2 to 5 minutes without looking away.
3. Don't judge or analyze; just witness yourself with curiosity.
4. Notice what emotions arise: perhaps discomfort, sadness, warmth, or resistance.
5. Stay present with yourself, breathing gently as you hold your own gaze.

MAKE IT YOURS

- Let your gaze relax and blur slightly if direct eye contact feels overwhelming.
- Gaze into one eye, then the other; notice which eye feels more comfortable.
- If critical thoughts arise, try softening your gaze and silently saying, "I see you," to redirect from evaluating to witnessing.

Petting Ritual

Physical contact with animals releases oxytocin in both you and the animal, creating mutual regulation. Petting at a slow, rhythmic pace activates your parasympathetic nervous system and lowers cortisol. Animals offer connection without judgment or demands; they don't need you to explain yourself. Research shows that petting animals reduces blood pressure, decreases anxiety, and provides the benefits of touch when human contact feels too complex or unavailable.

Use When: You feel touch-starved, disconnected, or need gentle, safe contact.

1. Spend time with a pet (yours or someone else's) that doesn't mind being touched.
2. Pet them slowly and intentionally, focusing on the texture of their fur or skin.
3. Notice their breathing, warmth, and the weight of them against you.
4. Stay present with the sensations rather than thinking about other things.
5. Continue for at least 5 to 10 minutes, letting the rhythm of petting soothe you both.

MAKE IT YOURS

- Try petting different animals to notice which ones regulate you most.
- Lie down with a pet resting on you, if possible, for deeper pressure and warmth.
- Notice how your breathing naturally syncs with the animal's rhythm.

Grounded Partnership

Sitting back-to-back with a safe person provides the benefits of co-regulation without the intensity of face-to-face contact. You can feel their presence, warmth, and breathing without having to perform or maintain eye contact. Your nervous systems regulate each other through physical proximity and the subtle communication of breath and posture. Research shows that synchronized breathing and physical contact with safe people activates oxytocin release and parasympathetic responses. You're literally holding each other up.

Use When: You're with someone safe and want connection without words or eye contact.

1. Sit on the floor or other firm surface back-to-back with someone you trust.
2. Let your spines rest against each other, feeling the contact and support.
3. Notice their breathing: the rise and fall of their back against yours.
4. Allow your breath to naturally sync with theirs, or maintain your own rhythm.
5. Stay here for 5 to 10 minutes, just being present with shared support.

MAKE IT YOURS

- Stay silent or talk softly, whatever feels connecting.
- Add gentle pressure by leaning more fully into each other's backs.
- Use this as a quiet way to reconnect after conflict or distance.

Trusted Voice Anchor

Parasocial relationships—one-sided connections with media figures—can provide real nervous system regulation even though the person doesn't know you. That's because your brain responds to familiar, trusted voices with the same mechanisms it uses for in-person relationships. The consistency and predictability of certain voices feels safe. Research shows that hearing familiar voices can activate reward centers and reduces stress hormones. You're borrowing someone else's regulated state through their voice.

Use When: You need connection but don't have access to safe people in real time.

1. Choose a voice you find calming and trustworthy, such as a favorite podcaster, audiobook narrator, social media creator, or teacher.
2. Listen to them speak for 10 to 20 minutes without multitasking.
3. Focus on their tone, rhythm, and the regulation you feel from their voice.
4. Let their calm presence help settle your nervous system.
5. Return to this same voice regularly to strengthen the association with safety.

MAKE IT YOURS:

- Notice which types of content (e.g., educational, storytelling, or casual chat) regulate you most.
- Try video instead of just audio if seeing facial expressions helps.
- Use this before bed, during difficult moments, or when you wake up anxious.

Eye Contact Practice

Sustained eye contact activates your social engagement system, releases oxytocin, and creates attunement between nervous systems. It allows you to truly see and be seen, which many people crave but rarely experience. Research shows that prolonged mutual gaze increases feelings of love, trust, and connection. This practice can bring up emotion because it breaks through the protective distance we usually maintain. But this discomfort is part of the reconnection—your nervous system remembering what true presence feels like.

Use When: You want deeper connection with someone safe but feel blocked or scared.

1. Sit facing someone you trust, at a comfortable distance.
2. Set a timer for 1 to 3 minutes.
3. Look into each other's eyes without speaking, allowing whatever arises.
4. If it becomes too intense, soften your gaze or look at their whole face rather than directly into their eyes.
5. When the timer ends, take a moment together before speaking about the experience.

MAKE IT YOURS

- Allow yourself to smile, cry, or laugh if emotions arise.
- Notice what it's like to be seen versus seeing the other person.
- Practice this regularly with someone you want to deepen connection with.

Growth Tending

Tending to plants reduces stress, increases feelings of connection, and can ease depression. Caring for living things activates your nurturing system and gives you purpose beyond yourself. Plants return the favor, responding to care in visible ways (e.g., growth, flowering, and health), which provide feedback that you matter and your actions have impact. Plants have a co-regulating effect simply through their presence and the responsibility they generate for gentle, consistent attention.

Use When: You feel purposeless, disconnected from life, or need to care for something.

1. Spend time tending to a plant: watering, pruning dead leaves, checking soil, and repotting when necessary.
2. Move slowly and notice the details such as new growth, texture of leaves, and moisture of soil.
3. Talk to the plant if that feels natural, or simply be present with it.
4. Recognize that this living thing depends on you and responds to your care.
5. Make this a regular practice, checking in on your plant daily or weekly.

MAKE IT YOURS

- Start with one easy-care plant if you're new to this: pothos, snake plant, or succulent.
- Keep the plant somewhere you'll see it daily as a reminder of connection.
- Notice how the plant's health reflects your capacity to show up for yourself.

Public Proximity

Your nervous system regulates through proximity to others, even without direct interaction. This is known as environmental co-regulation. This practice gently reintroduces social stimuli when you've been isolated, building tolerance for connection without the vulnerability of actual engagement. Research on loneliness shows that simply being around others, even strangers, reduces isolation and can lift mood. You're practicing being part of the world again without having to perform or explain yourself.

Use When: You've been isolating and need gentle reentry into the world of people.

1. Go to a public space where people gather, such as a coffee shop, library, park, bookstore, or even a train or bus.
2. You don't have to interact with anyone. Just be present in the same space.
3. Notice the ambient sounds, movement, and energy of other humans existing nearby.
4. Stay for 20 to 30 minutes, reading, working, or simply observing.
5. Let your nervous system remember what it feels like to be around people without pressure to engage.

MAKE IT YOURS

- Go during quieter times if crowds feel too overwhelming initially.
- Bring something to do (e.g., book, laptop, or knitting) so you have a focus beyond just sitting.
- Try different locations to find which environments feel most regulating.

Musical Connection

Music activates emotional and social brain regions simultaneously, making it a powerful vehicle for connection. Sharing music is an act of vulnerability; you're letting someone into your internal experience through sound. When someone receives and listens to your song, they're literally experiencing the same auditory patterns you chose, creating a form of shared experience even across distance. You're using art to strengthen social bonds and increase feelings of closeness.

Use When: You want to share something meaningful but don't have words for it.

1. Think of a song that captures something you're feeling or wanting to share.
2. Send it to someone you care about with a simple message like "This made me think of you" or "This is how I'm feeling today."
3. You don't need to explain why or provide context unless you want to.
4. Let the music communicate what words can't.
5. Notice how sharing something that matters to you creates connection, even without response.

MAKE IT YOURS

- Create a collaborative playlist with someone as an ongoing exchange.
- Consider sharing songs that express difficult emotions you can't voice directly.
- Notice which people appreciate your musical sharing, and deepen those connections.

PART III

Practice Plans and Personalization

In this part, we go from "that helped in the moment" to "this is actually changing how I move through my life." Here you'll find tools to build practices that fit into your real life—the one with interruptions, inconsistency, and days when nothing goes as planned. Let's make this work for you, step by (manageable) step.

CHAPTER 10

7-Day Reset Plan

During seasons of overwhelm, often the last thing we want to do is figure out which exercises to do and when to do them. So, I've done it for you. This chapter gives you a one-week map to begin building a practice that doesn't just change how you feel in the moment; it also takes small steps to rewiring your nervous system to become more flexible, less reactive, and more attuned to your needs.

You'll find three exercises per day: morning, midday, and evening. They are simple, manageable, and already decided. (Of course, you have the freedom to swap out something that better speaks to your individual needs.)

This isn't about transforming your entire life in seven days. It's about showing up for yourself consistently enough that your body starts to remember what it feels like to not be constantly activated or shut down. You're practicing relief until it becomes something more sustainable.

If a practice doesn't land, skip it and choose something different from that chapter. Miss a day? Pick up where you left off. No one is keeping score. The point is building some momentum without burning out or making this another thing you're failing at.

After this week, you'll know more about what actually works for your nervous system. Then you can repeat this, try the 30-day plan, or build your own approach entirely.

Seven days. You can do seven days. Let's get started.

DAY 1

Ground and Orient

Today is about coming back into your body and remembering where you are. We're using grounding, sensory awareness, and gentle movement to help your nervous system land after wherever it's been.

Morning Practice: Grounding Down (p. 41)

Pressing your feet activates proprioceptive receptors that send stability signals to your brain, helping you feel grounded and supported.

1. Sit or stand with both feet flat on the ground.
2. Press your feet firmly into the floor, as if making an impression.
3. Notice the sensation of the ground beneath you, the pressure in your feet.
4. Hold for 5 to 10 seconds, then release.
5. Repeat 3 to 5 times, feeling more anchored with each press.

Midday Practice: Color Hunt (p. 42)

Visual searching pulls your attention out of anxious thoughts and into the present moment.

1. Pause and look around your environment.
2. Find something red, blue, yellow, green, and one more color of your choice.
3. Really look at each one: Notice its shade, texture, and where it sits.
4. Let your breathing settle as you search.

Evening Practice: Deep Belly Breathing (p. 135)

Belly breathing engages your vagus nerve and tells your body it's safe to rest.

1. Lie down with one hand on your chest and one on your belly.
2. Breathe so your belly rises while your chest stays still.
3. Exhale slowly, feeling your belly fall.
4. Continue for 5 to 10 minutes.

REFLECTION

- Which practice felt most accessible today?
- Where, in your body, do you feel most grounded right now?

DAY 2

Discharge and Release

Today is about moving energy that's been stuck in your system. We're using movement, sound, and safe expression to help discharge activation and create space for what's next.

Morning Practice: Primal Shake (p. 111)

Animals shake to discharge stress naturally. This lets your body do what it's been wanting to do. Doing this in the morning clears whatever your system held on to overnight and sets the tone for the day ahead.

1. Get on your hands and knees on a soft surface.
2. Shake your whole body vigorously, like a dog shaking off water.
3. Let your head, shoulders, torso, and hips shake freely.
4. Continue for 20 to 30 seconds, then pause and notice how you feel.

Midday Practice: Forceful "HA" (p. 100)

This explosive breath and movement discharges fight energy in a safe, contained way.

1. Stand with feet hip-width apart, arms overhead.
2. Take a quick breath in, then swing your arms down while bending your knees.
3. Exhale sharply with a loud "HA!" from your belly.
4. Repeat 10 to 20 times quickly.

Evening Practice: Supine Spinal Twist (p. 132)

Gentle twists release physical and energetic holding patterns, helping you settle before sleep.

1. Lie on your back with knees bent, arms in a T shape.
2. Let both knees fall slowly to the right, shoulders staying down.
3. Turn your head to the left.
4. Hold 1 to 3 minutes, breathing deeply.
5. Switch sides.

REFLECTION

- What shifted after moving trapped energy today?
- Did discharge feel scary or relieving (or both)?

DAY 3

Slow and Settle

Today is about downregulating and helping your system remember it's safe to slow down. We're using breath, gentle movement, and restorative positions to ease you toward rest.

Morning Practice: Physiological Sigh (p. 125)

Taking a double inhale and long exhale is one of the fastest ways to calm your nervous system.

1. Take a deep inhale through your nose, filling your lungs about 80 percent.
2. Without exhaling, take a quick second inhale to top off completely.
3. Exhale slowly and fully through your mouth with a long sigh.
4. Repeat 2 to 3 times, feeling your body soften.

Midday Practice: Box Breathing (p. 110)

Box breathing balances your nervous system and regulates your heart rate through equal breath cycles. By midday, activation has usually stacked up—this clears the slate so you're not carrying the morning into the rest of your day.

1. Inhale through your nose for four, hold for four, exhale for four, hold for four.
2. Repeat 4 to 8 times, or until you feel your system shift.

Evening Practice: Legs up the Wall (p. 126)

This gentle inversion activates your parasympathetic system and drains tension from your legs.

1. Lie near a wall and scoot your hips close.
2. Extend your legs up the wall, with arms at your sides or on your belly.
3. Close your eyes and breathe naturally for 5 to 15 minutes.
4. To come out, bend knees and roll gently to one side.

REFLECTION

- What resistance, if any, came up when trying to settle?
- What does rest feel like in your body right now?

DAY 4

Connect and Belong

Today is about remembering that you exist in relationship to others and the world around you. We're using connection practices that feel safe and accessible, whether with yourself, nature, or other people.

Morning Practice: Intentional Smile (p. 150)

Smiling activates the same neural pathways as genuine joy and signals your nervous system toward openness.

1. Sit or stand and gently turn the corners of your mouth up into a soft smile.
2. Hold the smile for 30 to 60 seconds, even if it feels forced.
3. Notice any shifts such as warmth, lightness, or resistance.
4. Let it soften naturally, then try again if you want.

Midday Practice: Prosocial Messaging (p. 155)

Initiating social contact, even digitally, activates reward centers and moves you from isolation toward connection.

1. Think of someone you care about but haven't connected with recently.
2. Send them a simple message like "Just thinking of you," "Hope you're having a good day," or something you appreciate about them.
3. Send it without expecting a response.
4. Notice how reaching out shifts something in you.

Evening Practice: Tree Connection (p. 157)

Trees are living systems that your nervous system can co-regulate with, providing stability and connection.

1. Find a tree in your yard, in a park, or along a street.
2. Place your back against the trunk or your hands on the bark.
3. If it feels safe, close your eyes and notice the solidity and aliveness of the tree.
4. Stay for 3 to 5 minutes, letting yourself be supported.

REFLECTION

- Which type of connection felt most accessible today?
- What did you notice about reaching out versus receiving?

DAY 5

Rhythm and Restore

Today is about recognizing your body's natural patterns and working with them instead of against them. We're using rhythmic practices and restorative positions to help you find your groove.

Morning Practice: Rhythmic Drumming (p. 55)

Rhythmic movement organizes your nervous system and brings you into your body through predictable patterns.

1. Tap your thighs with your hands or a pen, imagining the beat of a drum.
2. Create any rhythm that feels good—fast, slow, offbeat, or steady.
3. Let the rhythm shift naturally as you play.
4. Continue for 2 to 5 minutes.

Midday Practice: Alternate Nostril Breathing (p. 138)

This balances the left and right hemispheres of your brain and creates a steady, calming rhythm that naturally regulates your nervous system.

1. Sit comfortably and use your right thumb to close your right nostril.
2. Inhale through your left nostril.
3. Close your left nostril with your ring finger, release your thumb, and exhale through your right nostril.
4. Inhale through your right nostril, then switch and exhale through your left.
5. Continue for 5 to 10 rounds.

Evening Practice: Constructive Rest (p. 136)

This position requires no muscular effort, allowing your body to completely release while gravity does the work of supporting you.

1. Lie on your back with knees bent and your feet flat and hip-width apart.
2. Let your knees lean gently toward each other for support.
3. Place arms at your sides or hands on your belly.
4. Stay for 10 to 20 minutes, breathing naturally.

REFLECTION

- What rhythms feel supportive versus chaotic?
- How does your nervous system respond to predictability?

DAY 6

Integrate and Strengthen

Today is about building capacity by layering what you've learned. We're using practices that require slightly more coordination or challenge you to stay present under mild pressure.

Morning Practice: 5-4-3-2-1 Grounding (p. 107)

This sensory inventory pulls you out of internal overwhelm and into external reality, building your capacity to orient even when activated.

1. Name five things you can see.
2. Name four things you can touch.
3. Name three things you can hear.
4. Name two things you can smell.
5. Name one thing you can taste.
6. Go slowly and really notice each one.

Midday Practice: Wall Push and Sigh (p. 108)

Pressing against resistance discharges activation safely, and the sigh releases held tension in your chest and throat. This builds capacity to handle pressure.

1. Stand facing a wall with your hands pressed firmly against it at shoulder height.
2. Push into the wall with all your strength for 10 to 15 seconds.
3. Release and step back, letting out a big audible sigh.
4. Repeat 3 to 5 times.

Evening Practice: Progressive Muscle Relaxation (p. 128)

This practice teaches your body the difference between holding and letting go and helps build awareness of where you carry tension.

1. Lie down and systematically tense each muscle group for five seconds, then release.
2. Start with your toes, then move through your legs, core, arms, shoulders, and face.
3. Notice the contrast between tension and release in each area.
4. Continue through your whole body over 10 to 15 minutes.

REFLECTION

- Where did you want to quit or disconnect, and what helped you stay?
- How has your capacity shifted over the week?

DAY 7

Rest and Reflect

Today is the gentlest day; it's about consolidating what you've learned and honoring how far you've come. We're using the softest, most restorative practices available.

Morning Practice: Gentle Rocking (p. 53)

Rhythmic rocking is one of the oldest forms of self-soothing. The gentle, repetitive motion calms your nervous system and can help you feel held and safe.

1. Sit on the floor or in a chair with your feet on the ground.
2. Begin rocking gently forward and back or side to side.
3. Let the movement be small and slow, like a metronome.
4. Close your eyes if that feels safe.
5. Continue for 3 to 5 minutes, letting the rhythm soothe you.

Midday Practice: Humming (p. 61)

Humming stimulates the vagus nerve through vocal vibration and creates a gentle, internal massage. The sound and sensation help bring you back into your body.

1. Sit comfortably with your lips closed.
2. Take a breath in through your nose.
3. As you exhale, hum at any pitch that feels comfortable.
4. Feel the vibration in your face, throat, and chest.
5. Continue for 2 to 3 minutes, humming on each exhale.

Evening Practice: Supported Child's Pose (p. 144)

This gentle forward fold is deeply restorative. The compression on your front body and the support underneath signal complete safety and permission to rest.

1. Kneel on your bed or a soft surface with your knees wide apart.
2. Place a pillow, bolster, or folded blankets under your torso for full support.
3. Extend your arms forward or rest them alongside your body.
4. Stay for 3 to 10 minutes, breathing into the back of your body.
5. Can't get into this position? Lie on your back and hug your knees gently toward your chest, or curl up on your side with a pillow to hold.

REFLECTION

- Which practices will you continue and why?
- What did you learn about your nervous system that surprised you?

CHAPTER 11

30-Day Resilience Builder

Here's the thing about nervous system work: Relief is great, but resilience is better. This chapter gives you a full month to build real, lasting capacity, the kind that doesn't disappear the moment life gets hard again.

This isn't a rigid program you have to follow perfectly. It's organized by weekly themes—Breath, Movement, Rhythm, and Connection—that guide you from dysregulation toward safety and social engagement. Each week builds on the last, but if you miss a day or need to repeat a practice, that's fine. Your nervous system learns through consistency, not perfection.

You'll practice one exercise per day. Some might feel easy. Others might feel impossible. Both are useful information. The weekly check-in prompts help you notice what's changing in your body and your life as new patterns take root.

Five minutes a day, practiced regularly, creates more lasting change than occasional marathon sessions. This is about building a relationship with regulation, not checking boxes. If a week's theme doesn't land, move to the next one. If an exercise resonates, repeat it. Trust that every practice is teaching your system something about what safety and flexibility feel like.

Miss a day or five? Start again tomorrow. Your nervous system is more forgiving than you think.

WEEK 1

Breath

This week focuses on using breath as your primary tool for nervous system regulation. Breath is the fastest, most accessible way to shift your state, and these seven practices will teach you how to breathe your way through activation, shutdown, and everything in between.

Day 1: Extended Exhale (p. 49)

Extending your exhale activates the parasympathetic nervous system and stimulates the vagus nerve, naturally slowing your heart rate and bringing you out of fight-or-flight activation.

1. Sit or stand comfortably, letting your shoulders relax.
2. Inhale through your nose naturally and count how long that takes.
3. Exhale through your mouth (or nose) for 1 to 2 counts longer than your natural inhale.
4. Pause naturally before your next inhale.
5. Repeat for 5 to 10 breaths, making each exhale longer than your inhale.

REFLECTION: *What changed in your body after just 5 to 10 breaths?*

Day 2: Box Breathing (p. 110)

Box breathing balances your nervous system and regulates your heart rate through equal breath cycles.

1. Inhale through your nose for four, hold for four, exhale for four, hold for four.
2. Repeat 4 to 8 times, or until you feel your system shift.

REFLECTION: *When you held your breath, where did you feel the stillness in your body?*

Day 3: Physiological Sigh (p. 125)

Taking a double inhale and long exhale is one of the fastest ways to calm your nervous system.

1. Take a deep inhale through your nose, filling your lungs about 80 percent.
2. Without exhaling, take a quick second inhale to top off completely.
3. Exhale slowly and fully through your mouth with a long sigh.
4. Repeat 2 to 3 times, feeling your body soften.

REFLECTION: *Did the sigh feel releasing or vulnerable?*

Day 4: Straw Breathing (p. 114)

The restricted exhale creates back-pressure that slows your breathing rate and activates a calming nervous system response.

1. Purse your lips as if drinking through a straw.
2. Inhale normally through your nose.
3. Exhale slowly through pursed lips, controlling the flow of air.
4. Make the exhale last 6 to 8 counts.
5. Repeat for 10 to 15 breaths.

REFLECTION: *How does controlling your breath affect your sense of control overall?*

Day 5: 4-7-8 Breathing Pattern (p. 134)

This pattern forces a slow, deliberate pace that signals safety and deep relaxation to your nervous system.

1. Exhale completely through your mouth.
2. Close your mouth and inhale through your nose for four counts.
3. Hold your breath for seven counts.
4. Exhale completely through your mouth for eight counts.
5. Repeat four cycles.

REFLECTION: *Where did you notice resistance to slowing down?*

Day 6: Left Nostril Breathing (p. 116)

Left nostril breathing activates your parasympathetic nervous system and has a cooling, calming effect.

1. Sit comfortably and use your right thumb to close your right nostril.
2. Inhale slowly through your left nostril.
3. Release and exhale slowly through your right nostril.
4. Continue for 5 to 10 breaths, keeping your right nostril closed.

REFLECTION: *How does breathing through one nostril change your experience?*

Day 7: Deep Belly Breathing (p. 135)

Belly breathing engages your vagus nerve and tells your body it's safe to rest.

1. Lie down with one hand on your chest and one on your belly.
2. Breathe so that your belly rises while your chest stays still.
3. Exhale slowly, feeling your belly fall.
4. Continue for 5 to 10 minutes.

REFLECTION: *What does it feel like to breathe fully into your belly instead of your chest?*

END-OF-WEEK CHECK-IN

- How has your relationship with your breath shifted this week?
- Where in your day could you integrate one of these practices regularly?

WEEK 2

Movement

This week focuses on using your body to discharge activation, shift stuck energy, and rebuild the connection between your mind and your physical self. Movement is medicine, and these practices range from gentle to vigorous.

Day 8: Ankle Circles (p. 57)

Gentle movement in your extremities wakes up your nervous system without overwhelming it.

1. Sit or lie down comfortably.
2. Lift one foot slightly off the ground.
3. Slowly rotate your ankle in circles: 10 in one direction, then 10 in the other.
4. Switch feet and repeat.

REFLECTION: *How does small movement create bigger shifts?*

Day 9: Primal Shake (p. 111)

Animals shake to discharge stress naturally. This lets your body do what it's been wanting to do.

1. Get on your hands and knees on a soft surface.
2. Shake your whole body vigorously, like a dog shaking off water.
3. Let your head, shoulders, torso, and hips shake freely.
4. Continue for 20 to 30 seconds, then pause and notice how you feel.

REFLECTION: *What did your body release that you didn't know you were holding?*

Day 10: Crossbody Punches (p. 94)

Crossbody movements integrate your left and right hemispheres while discharging fight energy safely.

1. Stand with feet hip-width apart, knees soft.
2. Punch your right fist across your body toward the left.
3. Return to center, then punch your left fist toward the right.
4. Build rhythm and speed, letting your torso rotate with each punch.
5. Continue for 1 to 2 minutes.

REFLECTION: *What came up for you when moving with force?*

Day 11: Head Rolls (p. 60)

Your neck holds enormous tension. Gentle rolling releases tightness and can shift your whole system.

1. Sit or stand with your spine long.
2. Drop your chin toward your chest.
3. Slowly roll your head to the right, letting it hang heavy.
4. Continue rolling your head back, then to the left, then return to center.
5. Repeat 3 to 5 times in each direction.

REFLECTION: *Where did you notice the most tension as you moved?*

Day 12: Arm Circles (p. 92)

Sustained arm movement activates your upper body and helps discharge restless energy.

1. Stand with feet hip-width apart.
2. Extend both arms out to your sides at shoulder height.
3. Make small circles forward for 30 seconds.
4. Reverse and make small circles backward for 30 seconds.
5. Gradually make the circles bigger, then smaller again.

REFLECTION: *Did your breathing change as you sustained the movement?*

Day 13: Stomp and Growl (p. 88)

Combining forceful movement with sound gives your fight energy a safe place to land.

1. Stand with feet hip-width apart.
2. Stomp one foot down firmly, then the other.
3. As you stomp, let out a low growl or grunt from your belly.
4. Continue stomping and growling for 30 to 60 seconds.
5. Pause and notice how your body feels.

REFLECTION: *What did it feel like to make noise with your movement?*

Day 14: Stand and Sway (p. 62)

The rhythmic side-to-side movement is naturally soothing and helps bring energy back into your body.

1. Stand with your feet hip-width apart, knees soft.
2. Begin swaying gently side to side, letting your weight shift from foot to foot.
3. Let your arms hang, or wrap them around yourself.
4. Close your eyes if that feels safe.
5. Continue for 3 to 5 minutes.

REFLECTION: *How does gentle movement feel different from forceful movement?*

END-OF-WEEK CHECK-IN

- Which movement practice felt most natural? Which surprised you?
- What movement wants to become part of your daily routine?

WEEK 3

Rhythm

This week focuses on creating patterns, rituals, and predictability. Your nervous system craves rhythm because it's organizing, orienting, and deeply regulating. These practices help you find your natural cadence.

Day 15: Rhythmic Drumming (p. 55)

Rhythmic movement organizes your nervous system and brings you into your body through predictable patterns.

1. Tap your thighs with your hands or a pen, imagining the beat of a drum.
2. Create any rhythm that feels good—fast, slow, offbeat, or steady.
3. Let the rhythm shift naturally as you play.
4. Continue for 2 to 5 minutes.

REFLECTION: *What rhythm did your body want to create?*

Day 16: Alternate Hand Squeezes (p. 67)

Alternating bilateral movements create rhythm and integration between your brain hemispheres.

1. Sit or lie down and make fists with both hands.
2. Squeeze your right hand for 3 seconds, then release.
3. Squeeze your left hand for 3 seconds, then release.
4. Continue alternating for 1 to 2 minutes, creating a steady rhythm.

REFLECTION: *Did the rhythm feel soothing or activating?*

Day 17: Percussion Reset (p. 81)

Clapping creates sound, rhythm, and physical sensation all at once, organizing multiple sensory channels.

1. Stand or sit comfortably.
2. Clap your hands together in any rhythm—steady, offbeat, fast, or slow.
3. Vary the volume and speed as you go.
4. Continue for 1 to 2 minutes.

REFLECTION: *How did creating your own rhythm affect your state?*

Day 18: Mobile Triangle Breath (p. 80)

Coordinating breath with movement creates a powerful organizing rhythm for your nervous system.

1. Inhale for three counts while taking three steps forward.
2. Hold your breath for three counts while standing still.
3. Exhale for three counts while taking three steps backward.
4. Repeat, creating a rhythm of breath and movement together.
5. Continue for 2 to 3 minutes.

REFLECTION: *What happened when you combined breath and movement?*

Day 19: Humming (p. 61)

Humming stimulates the vagus nerve through vocal vibration and creates a gentle, internal massage.

1. Sit comfortably with your lips closed.
2. Take a breath in through your nose.
3. As you exhale, hum at any pitch that feels comfortable.
4. Feel the vibration in your face, throat, and chest.
5. Try varying the pitch—higher, lower—and notice how different tones create vibration in different parts of your body.
6. Continue for 2 to 3 minutes, humming on each exhale.

REFLECTION: *Where did you feel the vibration most strongly?*

Day 20: Alternate Nostril Breathing (p. 138)

This balances the left and right hemispheres of your brain and creates a steady, calming rhythm.

1. Sit comfortably and use your right thumb to close your right nostril.
2. Inhale through your left nostril.
3. Close your left nostril with your ring finger, release your thumb, and exhale through your right nostril.
4. Inhale through your right nostril, then switch and exhale through your left.
5. Continue for 5 to 10 rounds.

REFLECTION: *How does the alternating pattern affect your focus?*

Day 21: Gentle Rocking (p. 53)

Rhythmic rocking is one of the oldest forms of self-soothing. The gentle, repetitive motion calms your nervous system.

1. Sit on the floor or in a chair with your feet on the ground.
2. Begin rocking gently forward and back or side to side.
3. Let the movement be small and slow, like a metronome.
4. Close your eyes if that feels safe.
5. Continue for 3 to 5 minutes, letting the rhythm soothe you.

REFLECTION: *What memories or feelings came up with this movement?*

END-OF-WEEK CHECK-IN

- Which rhythmic practice felt most grounding?
- How has creating patterns affected your sense of stability?

WEEK 4

Connection

This final week focuses on reconnecting with yourself, with others, and with the world around you. Connection is the ultimate sign of nervous system safety, and these practices help you remember that you belong.

Day 22: Acupressure Hug (p. 152)

Crossing your arms activates bilateral stimulation while pressure creates a sense of being held and safe.

1. Cross your arms and place each hand on the opposite shoulder.
2. Apply gentle, firm pressure as if giving yourself a hug.
3. Hold for 30 to 60 seconds, breathing slowly.
4. Add a gentle rocking motion if that feels good.

REFLECTION: *What does it feel like to hold yourself?*

Day 23: Prosocial Messaging (p. 155)

Initiating social contact activates reward centers and moves you from isolation toward connection.

1. Think of someone you care about but haven't connected with recently.
2. Send them a simple message like "Just thinking of you," "Hope you're having a good day," or something you appreciate about them.
3. Send it without expecting a response.
4. Notice how reaching out shifts something in you.

REFLECTION: *How did it feel to reach out without needing anything back?*

Day 24: Tree Connection (p. 157)

Trees are living systems that your nervous system can co-regulate with, providing stability and connection.

1. Find a tree in your yard, in a park, or along a street.
2. Place your back against the trunk or your hands on the bark.
3. If it feels safe, close your eyes and notice the solidity and aliveness of the tree.
4. Stay for 3 to 5 minutes, letting yourself be supported.

REFLECTION: *What did you notice about being near something alive and rooted?*

Day 25: Mirror Gaze (p. 158)

Meeting your own gaze builds self-connection and can reveal where you've been disconnected from yourself.

1. Sit in front of a mirror where you can see your whole face.
2. Look into your own eyes without judgment or criticism.
3. Stay for 2 to 5 minutes, just being with yourself.
4. Notice what comes up such as discomfort, softness, sadness, or warmth.

REFLECTION: *What did you see when you really looked at yourself?*

Day 26: Intentional Smile (p. 150)

Smiling activates the same neural pathways as genuine joy and signals your nervous system toward openness.

1. Sit or stand and gently turn the corners of your mouth up into a soft smile.
2. Hold the smile for 30 to 60 seconds, even if it feels forced.
3. Notice any shifts such as warmth, lightness, or resistance.
4. Let it soften naturally, then try again if you want.

REFLECTION: *What resistance came up when you tried to smile?*

Day 27: Nature Watching (p. 154)

Watching life unfold without an agenda activates calm alertness and reminds your nervous system that safety can include awareness.

1. Find a window, go outside, or look at a plant.
2. Watch something alive for five minutes without doing anything else.
3. Notice movement, color, texture, and the way light hits it.
4. Let yourself be curious rather than productive.

REFLECTION: *What did you notice that you usually miss?*

Day 28: Auditory Co-Regulation (p. 151)

Your nervous system naturally synchronizes with rhythmic, predictable sounds in your environment.

1. Play music, sounds of nature, or white noise.
2. Let the sound wash over you without doing anything else.

3. Notice how your breathing and body respond to the auditory input.
4. Stay for 5 to 10 minutes, letting the sound regulate your system.

REFLECTION: *What sounds help your body feel safe?*

Day 29: Eye Contact Practice (p. 162)

Sustained eye contact activates your social engagement system and builds intimacy and trust.

1. During a conversation with someone you trust, practice maintaining eye contact for slightly longer than feels comfortable.
2. Notice when you want to look away and see if you can stay present for one more breath.
3. Let yourself be seen.

REFLECTION: *What made eye contact feel difficult or easy?*

Day 30: Growth Tending (p. 163)

Caring for living things activates your ventral vagal system and reminds you that growth happens slowly with consistent attention.

1. Find a plant, garden, or any living thing you can care for.
2. Water it, prune it, notice its growth, or simply sit near it.
3. Spend 5 to 10 minutes tending to something alive.

REFLECTION: *What changed in you when you cared for something else?*

END-OF-WEEK CHECK-IN

- Which connection practice felt most meaningful?
- How has your capacity for connection shifted over this month?
- Of all four weeks—Breath, Movement, Rhythm, and Connection—which theme resonated most, and why?
- Looking at the past 30 days, how has your nervous system's capacity grown?
- Where do you still need support?
- Which practices will you carry forward?

CHAPTER 12

Build Your Own Practice Plan

You've learned the tools. You've tried the practices. Now it's time to figure out what actually works for your nervous system, your life, and your specific brand of dysregulation as it shows up today.

Here you'll find templates to track what helped, what didn't, and what patterns emerged when you paid attention. You're not looking for perfection here; you're looking for information. What shifted your state? What felt accessible on hard days? What surprised you by actually working?

These templates are designed to be flexible. Use the Go-To Exercises chart as your quick reference when you're dysregulated and can't think straight. Use the Daily Regulation Log to track individual practices as you experiment. Use the Weekly Practice Planner when you're ready to build more structure. Use the Monthly Reflection to zoom out and notice bigger patterns.

The goal isn't to fill out every template perfectly. The goal is to build self-knowledge, to become fluent in what your nervous system needs and when it needs it. Some people love tracking. Some people find it overwhelming. Use what serves you and leave the rest.

Go-To Exercises by Mood

This is your personal regulation cheat sheet for when your brain is too dysregulated to think. Fill it out now while you're calm, then keep it somewhere visible such as your phone, your fridge, or your bathroom mirror. Future you will thank you.

When I feel . . .	**I can try . . .**
Shutdown or frozen (chapter 4)	
Off or unclear (chapter 5)	
Angry or agitated (chapter 6)	
Anxious or overwhelmed (chapter 7)	
Need to sleep or settle (chapter 8)	
Need connection (chapter 9)	
Not sure/need a quick reset (chapter 3)	

TIP: Start with one practice per mood and add more as you discover what works. This is your personal regulation menu; build it over time.

Your regulation practice should feel like yours. These templates help you figure out what that looks like.

DAILY REGULATION LOG (p. 204)

These logs help you track what works for your nervous system. There are 30 days' worth on the following pages. Use them when you practice and you feel there is something noteworthy you want to remember or record. No one is grading you on whether you fill them out; this is a space for you to make mental notes, if and as they serve you.

TIP: Use symbols or just a few words to describe the shift. You don't need full sentences: "tight to looser" or "spinning to grounded" works perfectly.

WEEKLY PRACTICE PLANNER (p. 234)

When you're ready for more structure, these planners help you organize your practices without overwhelming yourself. Four weeks are laid out here, enough to start noticing what rhythms your body responds to.

TIP: Don't fill in the entire week ahead of time. Plan one day at a time based on what your body is telling you it needs.

MONTHLY REFLECTION AND TRACKER (p. 242)

Use these worksheets at the end of each month to zoom out and see the bigger picture. Two are included because patterns don't always show up in the first 30 days. Sometimes you need a little more time.

TIP: Look for patterns across multiple months. Your nervous system has rhythms: seasonal, hormonal, and relational. Tracking helps you anticipate and prepare.

Daily Regulation Log

Date:

Practice name:

How I felt before:

How I felt after:

Would I try it again? ☐ Yes ☐ No ☐ Maybe

Notes/insights:

Daily Regulation Log

Date:

Practice name:

How I felt before:

How I felt after:

Would I try it again? ☐ Yes ☐ No ☐ Maybe

Notes/insights:

Daily Regulation Log

Date: ______________________

Practice name: ______________________

How I felt before: ______________________

____

____

How I felt after: ______________________

____

____

Would I try it again? ☐ Yes ☐ No ☐ Maybe

Notes/insights: ______________________

____

____

____

____

____

Daily Regulation Log

Date:

Practice name:

How I felt before:

How I felt after:

Would I try it again? ☐ Yes ☐ No ☐ Maybe

Notes/insights:

Daily Regulation Log

Date: ______________________

Practice name: ____

How I felt before: ____

____

____

How I felt after: ____

____

____

Would I try it again? ☐ Yes ☐ No ☐ Maybe

Notes/insights: ____

____

____

____

____

____

Daily Regulation Log

Date:

Practice name:

How I felt before:

How I felt after:

Would I try it again? Yes No Maybe

Notes/insights:

Daily Regulation Log

Date: ______________________

Practice name: ______________________

How I felt before: ______________________

____

____

How I felt after: ______________________

____

____

Would I try it again? ☐ Yes ☐ No ☐ Maybe

Notes/insights: ______________________

____

____

____

____

____

Daily Regulation Log

Date: ____________________

Practice name:

How I felt before:

How I felt after:

Would I try it again? ☐ Yes ☐ No ☐ Maybe

Notes/insights:

Daily Regulation Log

Date:

Practice name:

How I felt before:

How I felt after:

Would I try it again? ☐ Yes ☐ No ☐ Maybe

Notes/insights:

Daily Regulation Log

Date: ______________________

Practice name: ______________________

How I felt before: ______________________

____

____

How I felt after: ______________________

____

____

Would I try it again? ☐ Yes ☐ No ☐ Maybe

Notes/insights: ______________________

____

____

____

____

____

Daily Regulation Log

Date:

Practice name:

How I felt before:

How I felt after:

Would I try it again? ☐ Yes ☐ No ☐ Maybe

Notes/insights:

Daily Regulation Log

Date: ____________________

Practice name: ____________________

How I felt before: ____________________

____

____

How I felt after: ____________________

____

____

Would I try it again? ☐ Yes ☐ No ☐ Maybe

Notes/insights: ____________________

____

____

____

____

____

Daily Regulation Log

Date:

Practice name:

How I felt before:

How I felt after:

Would I try it again? ☐ Yes ☐ No ☐ Maybe

Notes/insights:

Daily Regulation Log

Date: ______________

Practice name: ______________________________

How I felt before: ______________________________

____

____

How I felt after: ______________________________

____

____

Would I try it again? ☐ Yes ☐ No ☐ Maybe

Notes/insights: ______________________________

____

____

____

____

____

Daily Regulation Log

Date: ____________________

Practice name: ____________________

How I felt before: ____________________

____

____

How I felt after: ____________________

____

____

Would I try it again? ☐ Yes ☐ No ☐ Maybe

Notes/insights: ____________________

____

____

____

____

____

Daily Regulation Log

Date: ____________________

Practice name: ____________________

How I felt before: ____________________

____

____

How I felt after: ____________________

____

____

Would I try it again? ☐ Yes ☐ No ☐ Maybe

Notes/insights: ____________________

____

____

____

____

____

Daily Regulation Log

Date: ______________________

Practice name: ______________________

How I felt before: ______________________

____

____

How I felt after: ______________________

____

____

Would I try it again? ☐ Yes ☐ No ☐ Maybe

Notes/insights: ______________________

____

____

____

____

____

Daily Regulation Log

Date:

Practice name:

How I felt before:

How I felt after:

Would I try it again? ☐ Yes ☐ No ☐ Maybe

Notes/insights:

Daily Regulation Log

Date:

Practice name:

How I felt before:

How I felt after:

Would I try it again? ☐ Yes ☐ No ☐ Maybe

Notes/insights:

Daily Regulation Log

Date: ______________________

Practice name: ______________________

How I felt before: ______________________

____

____

How I felt after: ______________________

____

____

Would I try it again? ☐ Yes ☐ No ☐ Maybe

Notes/insights: ______________________

____

____

____

____

____

Daily Regulation Log

Date: ____________________

Practice name: ____________________

How I felt before: ____________________

____

____

How I felt after: ____________________

____

____

Would I try it again? ☐ Yes ☐ No ☐ Maybe

Notes/insights: ____________________

____

____

____

____

____

Daily Regulation Log

Date:

Practice name:

How I felt before:

How I felt after:

Would I try it again? Yes No Maybe

Notes/insights:

Daily Regulation Log

Date: ____________________

Practice name: ____________________

How I felt before: ____________________

____

____

How I felt after: ____________________

____

____

Would I try it again? ☐ Yes ☐ No ☐ Maybe

Notes/insights: ____________________

____

____

____

____

____

Daily Regulation Log

Date:

Practice name:

How I felt before:

How I felt after:

Would I try it again? ☐ Yes ☐ No ☐ Maybe

Notes/insights:

Daily Regulation Log

Date:

Practice name:

How I felt before:

How I felt after:

Would I try it again? ☐ Yes ☐ No ☐ Maybe

Notes/insights:

Daily Regulation Log

Date:

Practice name:

How I felt before:

How I felt after:

Would I try it again? ☐ Yes ☐ No ☐ Maybe

Notes/insights:

Daily Regulation Log

Date: ____________________

Practice name: ____________________

How I felt before: ____________________

____

____

How I felt after: ____________________

____

____

Would I try it again? ☐ Yes ☐ No ☐ Maybe

Notes/insights: ____________________

____

____

____

____

____

Daily Regulation Log

Date: ______________

Practice name: ______________

How I felt before: ______________

____

____

How I felt after: ______________

____

____

Would I try it again? ☐ Yes ☐ No ☐ Maybe

Notes/insights: ______________

____

____

____

____

____

Daily Regulation Log

Date: ______________________

Practice name: ______________________

How I felt before: ______________________

____

____

How I felt after: ______________________

____

____

Would I try it again? ☐ Yes ☐ No ☐ Maybe

Notes/insights: ______________________

____

____

____

____

____

Daily Regulation Log

Date: ____________________

Practice name: ____________________

How I felt before: ____________________

____

____

How I felt after: ____________________

____

____

Would I try it again? ☐ Yes ☐ No ☐ Maybe

Notes/insights: ____________________

____

____

____

____

____

Weekly Practice Planner

This week's focus (e.g., grounding, connection, relaxation):

Monday

Morning:

Midday:

Evening:

Notes:

Tuesday

Morning:

Midday:

Evening:

Notes:

Wednesday

Morning:

Midday:

Evening:

Notes:

Thursday

Morning:

Midday:

Evening:

Notes:

Friday

Morning:

Midday:

Evening:

Notes:

Saturday

Morning:

Midday:

Evening:

Notes:

Sunday

Morning:

Midday:

Evening:

Notes:

Weekly Practice Planner

This week's focus (e.g., grounding, connection, relaxation):

Monday

Morning:

Midday:

Evening:

Notes:

Tuesday

Morning:

Midday:

Evening:

Notes:

Wednesday

Morning:

Midday:

Evening:

Notes:

Thursday

Morning:

Midday:

Evening:

Notes:

Friday

Morning:

Midday:

Evening:

Notes:

Saturday

Morning:

Midday:

Evening:

Notes:

Sunday

Morning:

Midday:

Evening:

Notes:

Weekly Practice Planner

This week's focus (e.g., grounding, connection, relaxation): ____________________

____

____

Monday

Morning: ____________________

Midday: ____________________

Evening: ____________________

Notes: ____________________

Tuesday

Morning: ____________________

Midday: ____________________

Evening: ____________________

Notes: ____________________

Wednesday

Morning: ____________________

Midday: ____________________

Evening: ____________________

Notes: ____________________

Thursday

Morning:

Midday:

Evening:

Notes:

Friday

Morning:

Midday:

Evening:

Notes:

Saturday

Morning:

Midday:

Evening:

Notes:

Sunday

Morning:

Midday:

Evening:

Notes:

Weekly Practice Planner

This week's focus (e.g., grounding, connection, relaxation):

Monday

Morning:

Midday:

Evening:

Notes:

Tuesday

Morning:

Midday:

Evening:

Notes:

Wednesday

Morning:

Midday:

Evening:

Notes:

Thursday

Morning:

Midday:

Evening:

Notes:

Friday

Morning:

Midday:

Evening:

Notes:

Saturday

Morning:

Midday:

Evening:

Notes:

Sunday

Morning:

Midday:

Evening:

Notes:

Monthly Reflection and Tracker

This month I wanted to feel:

Most helpful practices this month:

Patterns I noticed in my body:

Recurring feelings or emotions:

One small shift I want to try next month:

Monthly Reflection and Tracker

This month I wanted to feel:

Most helpful practices this month:

Patterns I noticed in my body:

Recurring feelings or emotions:

One small shift I want to try next month:

Resources

If you want to continue learning about nervous system regulation, trauma, and somatic practices, here are some resources that have informed my work and might support your journey:

BOOKS

Anchored by Deb Dana (Sounds True, 2021)

The Complex PTSD Workbook by Arielle Schwartz (Althea Press, 2016)

The Myth of Normal by Gabor Maté (Avery, 2022)

Waking the Tiger by Peter A. Levine (North Atlantic Books, 1997)

What Happened to You? by Bruce D. Perry and Oprah Winfrey (Flatiron Books, 2021)

ORGANIZATIONS AND HOTLINES

SAMHSA National Helpline: 1-800-662-HELP (4357) (free, confidential, 24/7)

Crisis Text Line: Text HOME to 741741 (free, confidential, 24/7)

Somatic Experiencing International: traumahealing.org

Polyvagal Institute: polyvagalinstitute.org

Your nervous system didn't learn dysregulation overnight, and it won't learn regulation overnight either. Be patient with yourself, find support when you need it, and remember that healing isn't linear.

References

Balban, Melis Y., et al. "Brief Structured Respiration Practices Enhance Mood and Reduce Physiological Arousal." *Cell Reports Medicine* 4, no. 1 (2023): 100895.

Breznoscakova, Dagmar, Milana Kovanicova, Eva Sedlakova, and Maria Pallayova. "Autogenic Training in Mental Disorders: What Can We Expect?" *International Journal of Environmental Research and Public Health* 20, No. 5 (2023):4344.

Coan, James A., Hilary S. Schaefer, and Richard J. Davidson. "Lending a Hand: Social Regulation of the Neural Response to Threat." *Psychological Science* 17, no. 12 (2006): 1032–39.

Dana, Deb. *Anchored: How to Befriend Your Nervous System Using Polyvagal Theory*. Sounds True, 2023.

Feldman, Ruth. "Parent-Infant Synchrony and the Construction of Shared Timing." *Journal of Child Psychology and Psychiatry* 48, no. 3–4 (2007): 329–54.

Gupta, Sharat, and Shallu Mittal. "Yawning and Its Physiological Significance." *International Journal of Applied and Basic Medical Research* 3, no. 1 (2013): 11–15.

Holt-Lunstad, Julianne, Timothy B. Smith, and J. Bradley Layton. "Social Relationships and Mortality Risk: A Meta-Analytic Review." *PLoS Medicine* 7, no. 7 (2010): e1000316.

Jo, Hyunju, Chorong Song, and Yoshifumi Miyazaki. "Physiological Benefits of Viewing Nature: A Systematic Review of Indoor Experiments." *International Journal of Environmental Research and Public Health* 16 (2019): 4739.

Kanber, Elise, Jonathan P. Roiser, and Carolyn McGettigan. "Personally Valued Voices Engage Reward-Motivated Behaviour and Brain Responses." *Social Cognitive and Affective Neuroscience* 20, no 1 (2025): nsaf056.

Levine, Peter A. *Waking the Tiger: Healing Trauma*. North Atlantic Books, 1997.

Li, Qian-Qian, Guang-Xia Shi, Qian Xu, Jing Wang, Cun-Zhu Liu, and Lin-Peng Wang. "Acupuncture Effect and Central Autonomic Regulation." *Evidence-Based Complementary and Alternative Medicine* 2013 (2013): 267959.

Maté, Gabor. *When the Body Says No: The Cost of Hidden Stress*. Vintage Canada, 2003.

Odendaal, J. S. J., and R. A. Meintjes. "Neurophysiological Correlates of Affiliative Behaviour Between Humans and Dogs." *Veterinary Journal* 165, no. 3 (2003): 296–301.

Park, Bum Jin, Yuko Tsunetsugu, Tamami Kasetani, Takahide Kagawa, and Yoshifumi Miyazaki. "The Physiological Effects of Shinrin-Yoku (Taking in the Forest Atmosphere or Forest Bathing)." *Environmental Health and Preventive Medicine* 15, no. 1 (2009): 18–26.

Perry, Bruce D., and Maia Szalavitz. *The Boy Who Was Raised as a Dog: And Other Stories from a Child Psychiatrist's Notebook*. Basic Books, 2006.

Porges, Stephen W. *The Polyvagal Theory: Neurophysiological Foundations of Emotions, Attachment, Communication, and Self-Regulation*. W. W. Norton & Company, 2011.

Schwartz, Arielle. *The Complex PTSD Workbook: A Mind-Body Approach to Regaining Emotional Control and Becoming Whole*. Althea Press, 2016.

Schwartz, Richard C., and Martha Sweezy. *Internal Family Systems Therapy*. 2nd ed. Guilford Press, 2019.

Sinha, Anant Narayan, Desh Deepak, and Vimal Singh Gusain. "Assessment of the Effects of Pranayama/Alternate Nostril Breathing on the Parasympathetic Nervous System in Young Adults." *Journal of Clinical and Diagnostic Research* 7, no. 5 (2013): 821–23.

Tarr, Bronwyn, Jacques Launay, and Robin I. M. Dunbar. "Music and Social Bonding: 'Self-Other' Merging and Neurohormonal Mechanisms." *Frontiers in Psychology* 5 (2014): 1096.

Thompson, Richard. "Gardening for Health: A Regular Dose of Gardening." *Clinical Medicine* 18, no. 3 (2018): 201–05.

Tramacere, Antonella. "Face Yourself: The Social Neuroscience of Mirror Gazing." *Frontiers in Psychology* 13 (2022): 949211.

Wever, Mirjam C. M., Lisanne A. E. M. van Houtum, Loes H. C. Janssen, et al. "Neural and Affective Responses to Prolonged Eye Contact with One's Own Adolescent Child and Unfamiliar Others." *Neuroimage* 260 (2022): 119463.

Exercise Index

WHEN YOU NEED A QUICK RESET/AREN'T SURE HOW YOU FEEL

WHEN YOU'RE SHUTDOWN OR FROZEN

WHEN YOU'RE OFF OR UNCLEAR

WHEN YOU'RE ANGRY OR AGITATED

WHEN YOU'RE ANXIOUS OR OVERWHELMED

WHEN YOU NEED TO SLEEP OR SETTLE

WHEN YOU NEED CONNECTION

About the Author

Melissa Romano, LGSW, is a licensed social worker and neurosomatic specialist who knows what it's like to feel stuck in survival mode because she's been there herself. Based in West Virginia, she developed the S.A.F.E. Method, a four-step framework for nervous system regulation.

Melissa holds certifications in applied polyvagal theory, yoga therapy, and integrative somatic trauma therapy. But what really drives her work is her approach to what she calls connected healing: the belief that regulation doesn't mean calm; it means connection. Connection to yourself, your body, your emotions, and the people around you, even when everything feels hard. Her philosophy is simple: You're not broken; you're protecting yourself. The problem isn't you; it's that your system got stuck in protection mode.

Melissa creates content that makes nervous system science feel less like a lecture and more like a conversation with someone who actually understands. She's known for disguising real therapeutic practices as viral challenges and meeting people exactly where they are, which is usually overwhelmed, exhausted, and wondering if healing is even possible.

Melissa is the author of *Vagus Nerve Deck: 75 Exercises to Reset Your Nervous System. Everyday Nervous System Regulation* is her first book. To learn more, visit ReclaimingHealthy.com.

Hi there,

We hope you found *Everyday Nervous System Regulation* helpful. If you have any questions or concerns about your book, or have received a damaged copy, please contact customerservice@penguinrandomhouse.com. We're here and happy to help.

Also, please consider writing a review on your favorite retailer's website to let others know what you thought of the book.

Sincerely,

The Zeitgeist Team